SHIPCARVERS
OF NORTH AMERICA

"Pocahontas", attributed to William Rush, ca. 1800-20. Courtesy Kendall Whaling Museum.

Shipcarvers
of
North America

by

M. V. Brewington

DOVER PUBLICATIONS, INC.
New York

Published in Canada by General Publishing Company, Ltd., 30 Lesmill Road, Don Mills, Toronto, Ontario.
Published in the United Kingdom by Constable and Company, Ltd., 10 Orange Street, London WC 2.

This Dover edition, first published in 1972, is an unabridged and corrected republication of the work originally published by Barre Publishing Company in 1962.

International Standard Book Number: 0-486-22168-7
Library of Congress Catalog Card Number: 79-187020

Manufactured in the United States of America
Dover Publications, Inc.
180 Varick Street
New York, N. Y. 10014

Contents

Illustrations

Preface

Wittth the decline of the wooden sailing vessel there passed into oblivion many of the arts of the sea. Of them all, perhaps the most to be regretted is that of the shipcarver, the half artist-half tradesman whose skill with the chisel gave so much of beauty and grace to the sailing ship. Once scores of these artisans were scattered through the seaports and shipbuilding centers; today probably not a single one can be found actively at work.

As in all things maritime, America had her share in this art. Indeed, one of the carvers attained fame not only in home ports but also in those of Europe and Asia. Actually little is known of most of our shipcarvers, and, considering the vast number of pieces that were carved, surprisingly few specimens or even records of the work have been preserved in public collections. Undoubtedly much survives in personal collections, in use as garden ornaments, or as architectural decorations. If these could be located, they would add much to our knowledge of the craft and the craftsmen.

The author is under no illusion that this study is a definitive history; the materials are far too widely scattered to permit any one man discovering half of them. But it is hoped the main thread of the story has been accurately traced. Quite likely there are omissions from the list of carvers; also there is doubtless evidence concerning specific work executed by known or unknown craftsmen which has not been found. I will appreciate having them brought to my attention.

For assistance in the preparation of this study I am indebted to Messrs. Louis Bolander, Julian P. Boyd, Alexander C. Brown, Holman Chaloner, William Bell Clark, Captain Andrew Davidhazy, Captain Wade De Weese, U.S.N., Ernest S. Dodge, Admiral E. M. Eller, U.S.N., Lawrence W. Jenkins, Commodore D. W. Knox, Francis B. Lothrop, Henri Marceau, Eric Muller, William Osgood, Philip Purrington, William A. Robertson, Henry Rusk, M. Vernon Safford, M.D., C. R. Sawyer,

Alton Skillin, Vernon D. Tate, D. Foster Taylor, Walter Muir White-hill, Charles M. Wright, "Captain Long John Silver", and Mesdames Dorothy C. Barck, Grace Jovejoy Faulkner, Evelyn W. Kendall and Phoebe P. Prime.

The color plate reproducing the figurehead "Pocahontas" used on the cover has been very generously provided by Mrs. Henry P. Kendall, The Kendall Whaling Museum, Sharon, Massachusetts.

M. V. Brewington.

Salem, Massachusetts.
1962.

I

The Early Years

SHIPCARVINGS depend primarily on a shipbuilding industry. In America, if the work done by the Spaniards be disregarded, the trade began in 1607 with the construction of the thirty ton pinnace *Virginia* at the mouth of the Kennebec River. After that modest start, thirteen years passed with nothing more than desultory small boat building. Then in 1620, realizing that "to hyer [ships] . . . will eat you out of all your profitt if not your principall" the Virginia Colony established the shipbuilding industry by importing twenty-five skilled shipwrights from England.[1] Eight years later the colony of Massachusetts Bay welcomed a group of six shipcarpenters from the Mother Country.[2] The French in Canada; the Dutch at New Amsterdam; the Swedes on the Delaware; the English in the other colonies; all began to build vessels. In the years between 1680 and 1714, Massachusetts alone owned 1300-odd native built vessels.[3] In 1700, New York had twenty-four ships; Boston had 194; and Maryland, three years before, had a merchant fleet of 160.[4] Although most of the vessels were small, many ranged in size up to 200 tons and larger. Not all carried figureheads to be sure, but the larger ones of all types did.[5] One can see this from clauses in the few extant contracts and bills for the construction of early vessels. In 1661, William Stevens, at Gloucester, Massachusetts, agreed to construct a ship for some British merchants, but the local representative of the owners had "to find all Iron work, carved work and Joiners [work]". A letter from a Barbados shipowner in 1671 to a New England agent ordering a "Catch" built at Piscataquay (Portsmouth, N.H.) instructed that she be "Set forth handsomely with Carved Work".[6] A contract dated 1695, at Charlestown, Massachusetts, specified "a pair of small quarter galleries" but stipulated the builder was not to supply the "carvers work".[7] Such contracts support Edward Randolph's assertion that Massachusetts produced "all things necessary for

1

shipping and naval furniture", and demonstrate that the specialized trades of shipwright, shipsmith, and shipcarver were already well established. But in some of the colonies, Maryland for instance, as late as the 1750's, carved work was still being imported, generally from New England.

Probably most of these first carvings were the work of either Edward Budd, Richard Knight, or of George Robinson, the only carvers thus far known to have been working in New England at the period.[8] The designs followed closely those currently in style at home in Old England not only because of tradition, but also because foreign styles of carvings could not become familiar to our artisans, thanks to the Navigation Acts which confined open trading with a few exceptions to British ports. Furthermore the craftsmen almost uniformly made their advertisements read: "Henry Burnett . . . Ship Carver from London . . ."[9] "Henry Crouch, Carver from London, now living in Annapolis Makes any sort of carved work for Ships";[10] "Philip Witherstone, carver from Bristol, Ship Carving done as Cheap as in England".[11]

The course of English figurehead carving during the first century of American shipbuilding was simple. In the reign of James I, ship decorations were used profusely with gilded carvings applied over almost the entire upper works of the hull. The principal piece was, of course, the figurehead; usually a lion on all except the very largest vessels of the Royal Navy. By the time of Charles II, the lion had become the standard pattern, and in 1703 that style was fixed by official regulation. The practice continued until 1727 when the "officers of H.M. yards . . . represented that different figures for the head may be more properly adapted for ornament . . . than a figure of a lion" and permission was granted to change the pattern on smaller vessels. Nevertheless the use of the "beast" to some extent continued well down to the 1760's.[12] As developments in naval architecture changed the contour of the knee of the head, the design of the lion varied considerably. Under James I, his body was almost horizontal, a lion passant (figure 1). Following the Restoration he became rampant, at times crowned (figure 2). From Queen Anne's time to that of George III, the lion rampant threw his head back and his chest out, a "lion braggart", one is tempted to say, as the power of the Royal Navy extended itself over the Seven Seas (figures 3 and 4).

Figure 2. Lion, period of William and Mary.

Figure 1. Lion, period of James I.

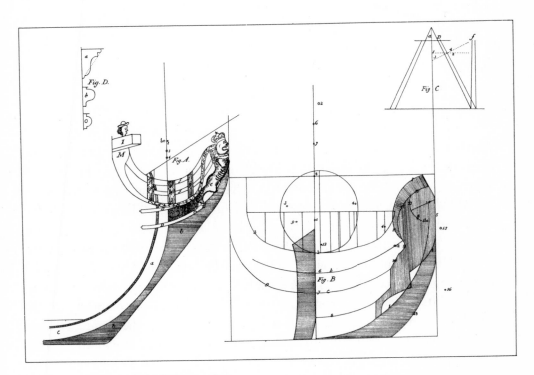

Figure 3. Lion, period of Queen Anne.

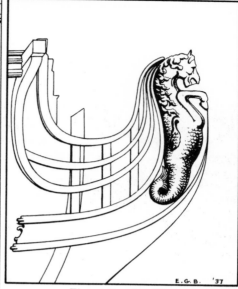

Figure 5.   Sea Horse, ca. 1760.

Figure 4.   Lion, period of George I.

The first definite knowledge of American figureheads appears towards the close of the seventeenth century. Then English practice unquestionably was followed. The earliest carver's bill so far found, that of Edward Budd and Richard Knight of Boston for the sloop *Speedwell*, 1689, called for a "Lyon" along with a "Tafferoll", "trailbor" and "bracketts". The "lyon" was, of course, the figurehead. On twelfth day, fourth month, 1700, Isaac Norris of Philadelphia wrote his English partner describing a ship, the *Pennsylvania Merchant* which was being built on the Delaware for the firm. Her carved work Norris listed as "Tafferil Lyon quarter ps".[13] Since no description of the piece is given in the letter, it can be safely assumed the head followed English practise so closely that none was necessary to inform the British partner about the appearance of that portion of the vessel's anatomy. None of the pieces was cut in Philadelphia, but all were ordered from a Boston carver whose name unfortunately is not mentioned in the letters.

Within a decade after this head was carved in Boston, Philadelphia had its own shipcarver, Robert Mullard. On the "17th Xbr 1708", he cut the carved work for the *Hope Galley* at a cost of £7.0.0.N.M. Following that doubtless among others he did the carvings for the *Greyhound Galley* (1711), the *Mary Galley* (1712), and the brigantine *Rachell* (1713);[14] all built at Philadelphia by James Parrock; all following English practise.

New York was apparently without a local carver many years longer than Philadelphia. Not until 1729 was "George Warburton, Carver", the first of his profession, admitted a freeman and allowed to practise his craft. Until then New England had been called on to supply the carvings for vessels built along Long Island Sound and the Hudson. For instance, the Salem Custom House books record, in 1714, the sloop *Union* clearing for New York with a "ships lyon" jammed into her hold along with an assorted cargo of sugar, molasses, hops, rum, a couch, 25 chairs, saddlery, and "sundry mackerel". The Rhode Island sloop *Beginning* carried another lion from Salem to New York.[15] Very probably all the carvings were the work of Leaman Beadle, one of the first

Figure 6. Figurehead of H.M.S. *America,* 1749. Courtesy Portsmouth Atheneum.

truly native American shipcarvers now known. Born in Salem, in 1680, Beadle spent his entire life span of thirty-seven years there, busying himself with all manner of architectural as well as ship carving.[16]

Shortly after Mullard began his work in Philadelphia, other carvers appeared. Several of their bills have been preserved, all furnishing evidence that Colonial carvings were following English fashions. In 1729 Anthony Wilkinson, a shipcarver living in Philadelphia charged Richard Deeble, "Mercht" £4.6.6. for "Carving a Lyon" for the new ship *Torrington*.[17] The next year for the snow *Delaware*, Wilkinson made a charge of £4.2.6. for "Carving a Lyon", and two years later he sent a bill to Dr. Richard Hill of Maryland "To cutting a lion 6 feet 4 Inches long at 14s pr ft £4.8.8.".[18] At about the same time William Hunt, another Philadelphia carver, was busying his chisels "carving the Lyon" for the ship *John and Anna*.[19] In 1748 Henry Wells acknowledged the receipt of "nine Pounds in full for Carving a Lion for the Ship *Mary*" just off the stocks in Benjamin Howell's shipyard at Marcus Hook.[20] Prints of the harbors of New York (1717), Boston (1725), and Philadelphia (1720, 1735, and 1751) all depict vessels which universally bore lion heads. The identical design was apparently current throughout the colonies: in the North, from the bills of Thomas More of Portsmouth, N.H. to William Pepperell in 1720 "to Carving a Lion 7½ feet Long att 14 pr feet" and if one may accept the evidence of the "lyon" figurehead of the model of the *America*, a vessel built at Portsmouth, N.H. about 1749;[21] in the South, since there was advertised for sale by Robert Morris at Oxford, Maryland, in 1745, "a neat carv'd Lyon's Head, fit for a ship of about 400 Hogsheads Burthen".[22] This last is of particular interest since Robert Morris was neither a carver nor a shipbuilder, but a "factor" who managed a large general store at Oxford. Evidently this head was a part of Morris's stock in trade. Carvers seem to have worked for inventory to some extent, as a statement of Joshua Bowles' losses in the great Boston fire of 1760 listed: "Three carved heads, one six foot and a half long, two, six foot long £60.".[23]

About the middle of the century just as the lion began to disappear in England, changes were taking place under the bowsprits of our vessels. A vessel lying in the harbor of Dunkirk in 1744 is described as "a New-England-built brigantine . . . with a horse's head".[24] A little later William Davenport, a Newburyport carver, billed a customer £9.0.0 for

Figure 7. Figurehead of Salem merchant ship, ca. 1750. Courtesy Peabody Museum of Salem.

Figure 8. Sea Horse figurehead, Newburyport merchant ship, ca. 1760. Courtesy Peabody Museum of Salem.

"a Sea horshead 6 foot long".[25] In 1756 the wreck of a brig reported in the Boston *Gazette* as wearing a "Horse head"; the next year a wrecked schooner carrying a "sea Horse head" was described.[26] Similar notations of the sea horse (figure 5) occur frequently, suggesting a definite vogue for it rather than the older lion.

By the middle of the 1760's animals of any kind seem to have passed out of style as figurehead motifs and human figures symbolizing the vessel's name began to appear in some numbers. Samuel Skillin once of Boston, and later of Philadelphia, for instance, billed James Wharton in 1765 "for Carved Work Don for the Brigg *Morning Star*, To a Venus head 7 feet long at 12 Shillings for a foot £4.18.0.".[27] A few years later the owners had affixed to the bow of the ship *Black Prince* (in 1775 to become the *Alfred*, the first flag ship of the Continental Navy) the image of that illustrious Englishman "Drawing a Sword".[28] The ship *Molly* (afterwards the Continental naval vessel *Reprisal*) carried a female figure, the portrait of her original namesake. Edward Cutbush of Philadelphia, "the best carver of his day . . . a man of spirited execution but of unharmonious proportions"[29] fixed a "King of Portugal" on the cutwater of the "ship being built of cedar" by Richard Dennis for Messrs Parr, Bulkely & Co of Lisbon;[30] and on the bow of the *General Putnam* built at New London, Connecticut, was carried a portrait figure of "Old Put" nine feet high.[31] None of the actual designs of these heads or others of the period seem to have been preserved.

Woefully little is known of the stern or other carvings used before the Revolution. The Budd and Knight bill of 1689 includes a "Tafferoll", or taffrail, but no clue is to be found concerning its design since we have not a single model, ship portrait or plan. This piece is defined as "the uppermost Part of a Ship's Stern Abaft, and always carved". Norris repeated the term in his description of the *Pennsylvania Merchant* of 1700 and added some additional evidence "quarter ps"—". . . two Pieces of Carved Work reconciled to each End of the Tafferel, and when regularly suited to the same with a just Disposition of Figures, completes the beautiful Symetry of the whole Stern . . .". The earliest known American attempt at ship portraiture, the sloop on the 1707 plat of Oxford, Maryland, shows neither;[32] the sloop in the Burgis view of Boston Light, 1728, shows both the taffrail and one quarter piece in profile.

8

Figure 9.   Stern of H.M.S. *America*, 1749. Courtesy Portsmouth Atheneum.

Figure 10.   Stern of Salem merchantman, ca. 1750. Courtesy Peabody Museum of Salem.

A comparison of these with English vessels of the same period seems to indicate that just as American figureheads followed the styles set in the Mother Country, stern carvings too, when used were in the same patterns. In fact, in the eighteenth century views of American ports it is impossible to distinguish between vessels of Western or Eastern Atlantic origin.

The earliest technical drawings of an American vessel are those of the sloop *Mediator* built in Virginia in 1741 and purchased by the Royal Navy in 1745. These plans show she had a simple cutwater without a knee or a figurehead, and that her stern had nothing more than windows in the transom.[33] A few years later the drawings of H.M.S. *Boston* built in Boston give the profile of the knee where a figurehead would be fixed, show fairly elaborate quarter galleries, and the outline of the transom but again none of the carvings are detailed.[34] This is true of all the now-known plans of American vessels built for or purchased by the British before 1775; if a figurehead was carried, its position only is indicated, and although the outline of the transom is given, nothing more than windows with a few mouldings appear. It is not impossible this type of stern was the more widespread. Mouldings could be cut by any joiner, and carvings being far more expensive, the simpler sterns would have had no small appeal to the thrifty. Certainly the plain stern is on the mid-eighteenth century model at the Peabody Museum, even though the model has a well carved figurehead and full quarter galleries (figure 10). There is no means of determining the frequency of the carved or plain stern because while ship registers at times mention the presence or absence of figureheads and galleries, those documents are always silent on stern decorations. The two mid-eighteenth century pieces of American evidence in which there are both figureheads and stern decoration — the model of H.M.S. *America* at the Portsmouth (N.H.) Atheneum, and the vessel in the duplicate paintings of the ship *Bethel* at the Adams Birthplace and at the Peabody Musum could all pass for British in every respect.

With quarter galleries and badges we fare better, typical designs are shown in figures 16-19. Both are taken from plans of American vessels in the Admiralty Collection.[35] When compared with either British or American plans of a half century later, it is obvious no changes had taken place at home or abroad.

Figure 11.   Quarter badge.

II

Independence

BEGINNING with the vessels of the Revolutionary period some positive knowledge of our ship decorations is to be found. In 1773 the British Admiralty ordered that a "complete draught with stern, head, and carved works sketched thereon" be made of vessels built or bought for the Royal Navy.[1] As many of the vessels captured from us were purchased into the British service, some of these draughts supply us with the designs of carvings carried by our vessels. Unfortunately the dockyards did not comply with the order in every case.

In those plans which have been preserved, the practise of carrying human figures symbolizing the vessel's name was continued. The first vessels built by the Continental Congress were thirteen frigates ordered in 1775 and laid down in 1776. Although the sizes and designs of each of these frigates were fixed by the Marine Committee, the carved work was left to the individual taste of each master shipwright as can be seen from a letter from John Hancock, a member of the Committee to Thomas Cushing, the superintendent of the two vessels built in Massachusetts. Hancock wrote, "let the heads & Galleries for the Ships be neatly carv'd and Executed, I leave the Device to you, but by all means let ours [those built in New England] be as good, handsome, strong & as early compleated as any building here in Philadelphia".[2] The designs of the figureheads of these frigates, built as they were from one end of the Colonies to the other represent a very accurate cross section of the best carving available in America at that time.[3]

One of the captured frigates was the *Raleigh,* built at Portsmouth, New Hampshire. She was taken off the coast of Maine in the fall of 1778 and at once bought into the Royal Navy. The draught made by the Admiralty shows her head perfectly: an effigy of Sir Walter Raleigh with a face heavily bearded, a body dressed in the carver's conception of the doublet, stockings, sashes and corselet, sword in hand,

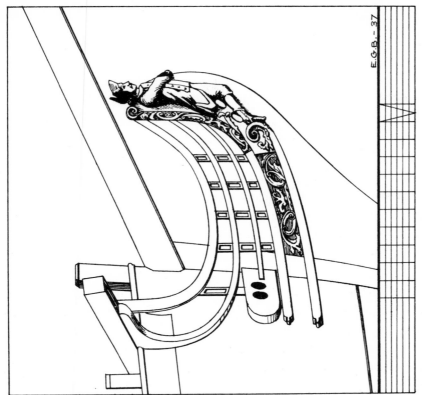

Figure 13. Figurehead of Continental Frigate *Hancock*, 1776. From plans in the Admiralty Collection.

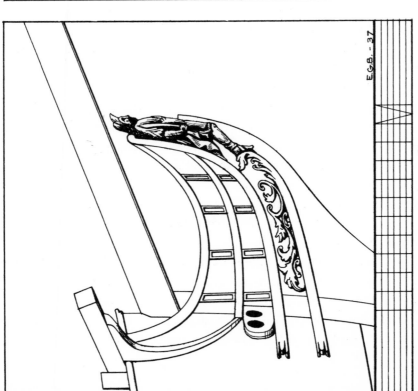

Figure 12. Figurehead of Continental Frigate *Raleigh*, 1776. From plans in the Admiralty Collection.

and steel casque on his head (figure 12).[4] Although there is no direct evidence concerning the carver who executed this head, very possibly it was William Deering, who at that time was the only shipcarver known to be living in or near Portsmouth. Deering was born in 1741, the son of William Deering, Senior, a noted architectural carver and builder. The younger Deering was undoubtedly trained by his father and very likely was working at the trade by 1763 since in that year he was married.[5] A short time after the frigate *Raleigh* was completed, Deering enlisted in the 12th Massachusetts Regiment and served as a sergeant until 1780 when he was honorably discharged. From his few extant letters he seems to have had a large number of commissions, not only in Portsmouth, but in all the nearby ports. None of his actual shipcarvings have apparently been preserved. In fact the only large identified piece of his work is the handsome bas-relief of the Good Samaritan in the Boston Dispensary, carved in 1790 for Benjamin Dearborn. Among the work definitely known to have been executed by Deering were the heads for the U.S. ship *Merrimack*, 1798, and the U.S. brig *Warren*, 1799.[6]

Another Continental frigate built at Newburyport was named *Hancock*. Her head was a full length portrait of John Hancock,[7] president of the Congress, wearing "yellow Breeches, white stockings, Blue Coat with Yellow Button Holes, small cocked Hat with a Yellow Lace"[8] (figure 13). Still another Massachusetts built frigate, the *Boston,* wore the figure of one of the original inhabitants of the Massachusetts Bay Colony: "An Indian with a Bow and Arrow in the Hand", according to a description given by a British spy.[9] Since the Indian was later to become a favorite motif for American shipcarvers it is to be regretted the design of the first known of the tribe of wooden redmen has not been preserved. But thanks to the Royal Navy's capture of the privateer *Rattlesnake,* a head on the same theme, cut just a few years later, 1781, has come down to us (figure 14). Her head was a full length statue of an Indian, possibly symbolizing in the carver's mind something equally as American as this reptile, or possibly the actual portrait of an aborigine of that name.[10] Ten more frigates were built at the same time as the *Raleigh, Hancock* and *Boston,* one group named for persons distinguished in our history: *Washington, Montgomery, Randolph, Trumbull, Effingham* and *Warren.* Each of these heads doubtless represented the person honored. The other frigates were named for the

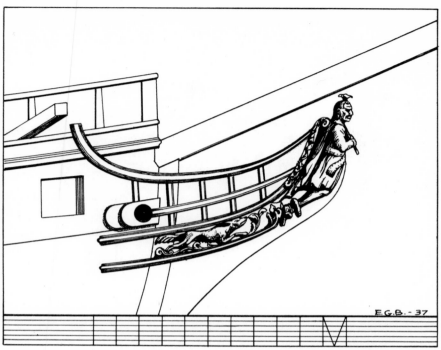

Figure 14. Figurehead of American privateer *Rattlesnake,* 1781. From plans in the Admiralty Collection.

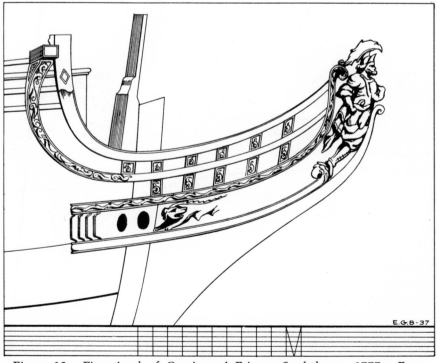

Figure 15. Figurehead of Continental Frigate *Confederacy,* 1777. From plans in the Admiralty Collection.

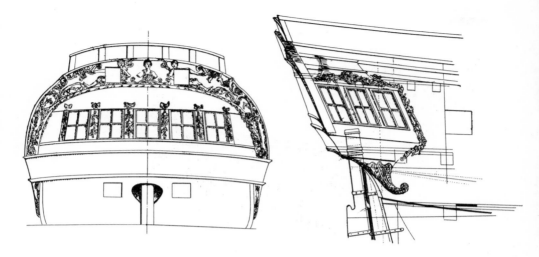

Figure 16.　Stern of Frigate *Raleigh*.　From plans in the Admiralty Collection.

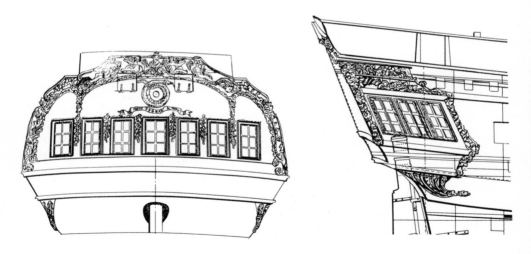

Figure 17.　Stern of Frigate *Hancock*.　From plans in the Admiralty Collection.

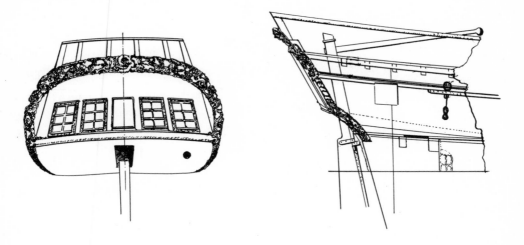

Figure 18. Stern of Privateer *Rattlesnake*. From plans in the Admiralty Collection.

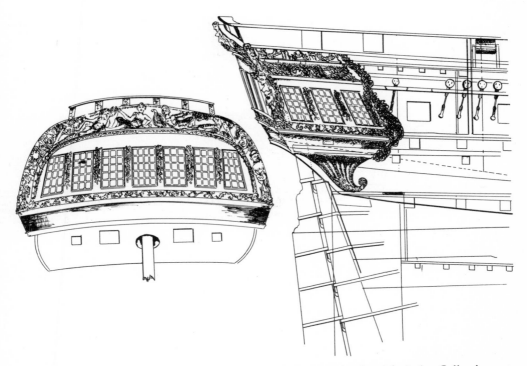

Figure 19. Stern of Frigate *Confederacy*. From plans in the Admiralty Collection.

city of *Providence*, the states of *Virginia* and *Delaware* and for the *Congress*. Despite the capture of all three of this last group and their subsequent entry into the Royal Navy none of their figurehead designs has been preserved in either line or word. Hence it is impossible to determine how the Continental carvers treated such names symbolically.

The next group of vessels built officially comprised the frigates *Alliance, Confederacy* and *Bourbon*. Of the second, launched at Norwich, Connecticut, in 1778, and captured in 1781, we have not only the design itself but also the name of the man who carved it. The figure was that of a warrior of the Greek Confederation in breast plate and plumed helmet (figure 15) the work of John Skillin,[11] a member of a remarkable family of shipcarvers whose work seems to have enjoyed wide popularity in several of the major seaports of the Colonies during the late eighteenth century.

So important was the Skillin dynasty of shipcarvers that something of its story must be recorded. Sometime prior to 1737, two brothers, John and Simeon Skillin, appeared among the maritime artisans in Boston. John was a shipcarpenter by trade and has no part in this story; Simeon was a shipcarver and has. For almost fifty years Simeon, born 1716 died 1778, worked in Boston, probably turning out "lyons" and other "beasts", all more or less like those from every other carver's shop. The earliest known ship carving by Simeon was mentioned in a bill for the *King George* dated January 2, 1758, signed "Skilling & Comp. Carvers". More important than his work, however, was the training he gave to his sons and relatives. Simeon had several children, among them three sons, John, Simeon [Jr.], and Samuel, who learned the father's trade. About 1765 Samuel struck out for himself and moved to Philadelphia where he married Elizabeth Towson and the next year had a son whom he named Simeon [III]. During the Revolutionary War Samuel executed the carved work for several Pennsylvania State Naval vessels, the carvings for two row gallies, a "Sea nymph" for the brigantine *Convention* among others, and also the work for numerous privateers, such as Joseph Carson's *Sturdy Beggar*. Then after serving in the Second Philadelphia Militia, he returned to Boston in time to be entered in the 1780 tax list. He appears to have remained in his birthplace working at his craft until his death in 1830. Of his work and ability we know little: only one of his bills seems to have been preserved, that for the ship *Lucy* of Kingston in 1806.[12]

Doubtless Samuel trained his son Simeon [III] whose time of apprenticeship would have run by 1788. Evidently Simeon was as footloose as his father for in the New York City Directories his name appears in 1792 and annually until 1830 when he died, the same year as his father. He had ceased carving by 1822 when he entered the crockery business. In 1793 a "John" is listed in the carving business with him. Who he may have been has not been discovered. Perhaps Boston John, his uncle, may have spent a year in New York.[13] Many of Simeon's [III] bills have been preserved, showing that he carved extensively for Connecticut as well as New York shipbuilders.

By the outbreak of hostilities with England, John and Simeon Jr. were well established in Boston and it would appear, had a virtual mo-

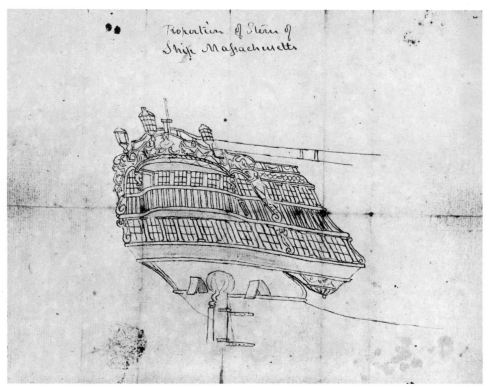

Figure 20. Stern designed by S. Skillin for merchant ship *Massachusetts*, 1789. Courtesy New York Public Library.

nopoly of shipcarving in and around Massachusetts and were in demand for important work from New Hampshire to Connecticut. They
executed such work as the head for the Continental frigate *Confederacy*
built at Norwich, Connecticut, 1778, for the privateer *General Putnam*
at New London, and for the Massachusetts naval brig *Hazard* at Boston, 1777.[14]

After the war John's and Simeon's business continued to expand as
the merchants, turning from privateering to trading, built up the great
fleet of vessels to dispatch to all the Seven Seas and take the world's
carrying trade. Men such as Elias Hasket Derby, the greatest merchant
and richest man of his time, came to the Skillins for practically all of
their important work, leaving the small carvings for lesser men. A splendid example of the Skillins' work is to be found in the stern of East
Indiaman *Massachusetts*, built in 1789, at Germantown, Massachusetts.[15]
The design signed "S. Skillin" has been preserved. When the frigate
Constitution was launched in 1797 on her bow she carried "An Hercules
with the fasces of the United States & the Constitution standing upon
a rock & his batoon lying beneath him".[16] This design was by William
Rush; the execution by the Skillins.[17] John died in 1800; his sudden
death causing the diarist Bentley who knew him to write, "This man has
long been known in this carving, particularly by our Seamen in all our
Seaport Towns".[18] At a later time Bentley called John a genius. The other
brothers, Simeon and Samuel, independently continued carving until
their deaths in 1806 and 1830 respectively. Of Simeon Jr., it is said,
"Such was his genius that he might be called an artist rather than an artisan. . . . Most of the figureheads that issued from the port of Boston
for many years were made by Mr. Skillins." (Figures 15, 19, 24, 30).[19]

In addition to the portrait style of figurehead the use of classical
mythology and history also is to be found in the heads of the Revolutionary period. Simeon Skillin Jr., of Boston, carved the head of the
Massachusetts State brig *Hazard*, built by John Peck and originally intended to be named the *Minerva*. Skillin's bill reads in part "To a Minerva Head 6 feet, 9 Inches £6.0.0.". The famous old Roman general Belisarius, in full armor and gear stood at the bow of the privateer of the
same name.[20] Similarly a Connecticut State cruiser carried the Roman
goddess of the chase, Diana.[21] The head for this vessel was sold to the
State by Ralph Isaacs of New Haven,[22] another example of a merchant

carrying ready-made heads in stock. In Philadelphia Samuel Skillin cut ı Nereid for the Pennsylvania Naval brigantine *Convention*.[23] Perhaps the proximity of the principal seats of classical learning, Harvard, Yale, and Pennsylvania to these seaports had some influence on the town as well as the gown.

Probably the most ornate piece of carving and certainly the heighth of symbolism in figureheads was attained on the ship of the line *America* launched at Portsmouth, New Hampshire, in 1782, and presented to the King of France. John Paul Jones, her prospective commander, exercising his facile pen and agile imagination described it: "a female figure crowned with laurels, the right arm raised with fore finger pointing to heaven as if appealing to that high tribunal for the justice of the American cause. On the left Arm was a buckler with a blue ground and 13 stars. The legs and feet of the figure were covered here and there with wreaths of smoke to represent the dangers and difficulties of the war".[24] Who executed this masterpiece is not certain, possibly William Deering, who, it is known, was in Portsmouth during the time when the work should have been under way. Probably it was John Skillin, at least the Navy Board of the Eastern District promised John Langdon, the *America*'s superintendent, on April 20 to "confer with Mr. Skillin about a suitable figure for the head of the 74 [gun ship]", and tentative arrangements to bring large pieces of timber to Boston were made for Skillin.[25] If the workmanship was on the same plane as the Commodore's conception, the figurehead would have been well worthy of its place in the French Fleet, along with those designed by the artists of the school of Puget.

Probably the work was not, for as can easily be seen from the reproduction of the contemporary American designs, there was very little grace in them. In all instances the heads seem to have been applied to each side of a solid knee, as a piece of high relief rather than as a full-round figure. All of them are stiff, mathematical in execution, following the contours of the knee and becoming a full figure only above the waist. They are utterly lacking in any semblance of freedom, or life, or of motion. One might be led to suppose their woodenness was due to poor drawing on the part of the English naval draughtsmen who sketched them, were it not for the further evidence of the contemporary method of attaching the head.[26] This is found in the splendid model of a seventy-

Figure 21. Figurehead of proposed Continental 74-gun ship. Courtesy Philadelphia Maritime Museum and U.S. Navy.

Figure 22. Stern of proposed Continental 74-gun ship. Courtesy Philadelphia Maritime Museum and U.S. Navy.

four gun ship made by Joshua Humphreys in 1777 for the Continental Marine Committee and also in what is perhaps the oldest actual figurehead preserved in this country, the little lady now in the Peabody Museum.[27] The first had for a head the image of a man, but since the vessel was not built or named, we have no idea who is portrayed or what is symbolized. Every detail of clothing and anatomy is carefully worked out in the figure, but there is the same hardness of posture found in the Admiralty draughts, and the figure is applied to the knee in precisely the same manner shown in the *Hancock, Raleigh,* and other Revolutionary drawings. The Peabody Museum figurehead, according to the catalog of its Marine Room, is "said to have been made by Samuel McIntire", the famous Salem carver "about 1800" (figure 23). Since the figure was acquired at the sale of McIntire's property, the attribution has some foundation.[28] It is only two feet long and must have been carved for a small vessel, possibly one of the little sloops or schooners that carried so much of the early coasting trade or possibly for the carver's shop sign. This head shows exactly the elements of design found in the figureheads of the Revolutionary period, the same mathematical position, the same crudeness in handling the draperies, and precisely the same manner of placing the image astride the knee in high relief becoming full-round only above the waist. At a later date after another style had been developed this type was termed by carvers a "straddle" head.

Both the McIntire figurehead and the head on the Humphreys model conclusively support the style of the pieces found in the drawings of the Revolutionary period. Other examples are to be seen in the model of the merchant ship at the Peabody Museum and an unidentified figurehead owned by the State Street Bank in Boston (figures 7 and 24).

Bridging the designs of the Revolutionary vessels with their continued dependence on English prototypes and the period when American shipcarving began to take on a style of its own was the highly publicized carver Samuel McIntire of Salem. As an architectural designer and decorator, as a furniture carver, all agree he ranked with the best in the United States in his time. A vast amount of his actual work in these fields has been preserved and a large number of his designs ranging from furniture parts to plans for the Capitol building at Washington are known, but only one attributed piece of shipcarving and a

Figure 23.   Figurehead attributed to Samuel McIntire. Courtesy Peabody Museum of Salem.

Figure 24. Figurehead attributed to Samuel Skillin.
Courtesy State Street Bank and Trust Co.

few designs have come down to us. Therefore it is difficult to evaluate his place as a shipcarver.

Samuel McIntire was born in Salem in 1757, the son of a house carpenter Joseph McIntire who trained his three sons in the same trade.[29] In 1802 Bentley, an able critic who knew Samuel well wrote of him, "As a Carver we place Mr McIntire with [Simeon] Skillings of Boston. In some works he succeded well. He cuts smoother than Skillings but he has not his genius. In Architecture he excells any person in our country and in his executions as a Carpenter, or Cabinet Maker".[30] But what of his sea-going work? Bentley is silent, although as we have seen he sang Skillin's praise as a shipcarver. McIntire's first known job of that kind was in 1776 at the age of nineteen, work done with one of his carpenter brothers, Joseph Jr., for Captain Tucker's schooner *Harliquin*. In the bill for the job no carving is mentioned and it is probable the work which took a total of 33¾ man-days consisted entirely of cabin joiner work. Except for a carved knee in 1789, until 1798 no bill has been found for much other than cabin bulkheads and the like. Then McIntire did all the carvings for the ship *Mount Vernon*, including a figurehead with its brackets and trailboards and stern and quarter galleries. The next year he executed all the work for the frigate *Essex* and in 1802 that for the brigantine *Pompey;* 1803, the ship *Asia;* 1806, the ship *Derby.*[31] Even though these bills can only represent a small portion of the work McIntire did for vessels, he must not have been considered a first rate shipcarver by his contemporary townsfellows for Elias Hasket Derby, one of McIntire's best architectural customers, called on the Skillins in Boston for much of his ship work, just as he did for the full figures on his famous "Tea House" which McIntire himself had designed.[32]

Several of McIntire's designs for shipcarvings have been preserved, among them twelve drawings for stern decorations, four for trailboards, two for full figureheads and two for billet heads.[33] All those for sterns and trailboards make one think McIntire simply transferred sofa backs and domestic architectural details to vessels. None show any originality. In fact, quite the reverse since one design for the stern on an uniden-tified vessel has pasted to it the printed "mast head" cut from the *American Federalist,* a spread eagle. Perhaps this is an indication of his own good taste because his own full-round eagles — many still exist — look more like scrawny roosters caught out in a downpour than our

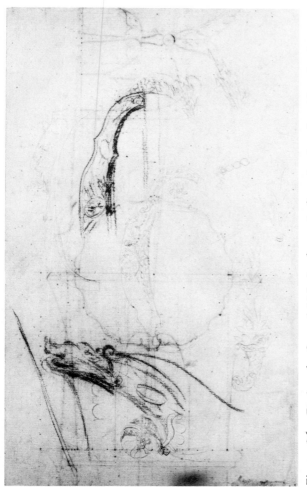

Figure 26. Designs by Samuel McIntire for eagle figurehead and archboards. Courtesy Essex Institute.

Figure 25. Designs by Samuel McIntire for figurehead of *Belisarius*(?), trailboards and stern decorations. Courtesy Essex Institute.

Figure 27. McIntire's design for stern of unidentified vessel. Courtesy Essex Institute.

Figure 28. McIntire's design for stern of unidentified vessel. Courtesy Essex Institute.

28

national symbol. Of the two designs for figureheads, a standing eagle and a Roman warrior, both in the full-round style introduced when McIntire was at the height of his career, neither has strength, both are as static as Gibraltar. When he died in 1811 among his effects was found "1 book drawings of ships" which was offered at the sale advertised in the Salem *Gazette*.[31] Probably it was one of the two books on shipcarving designs published in England at the turn of the century. But if so, his own designs certainly fail to show he profited by any study of the book. In short, McIntire, whatever his fame may have been ashore, on the now known evidence, does not rise as a shipcarver to the level of William Rush of Philadelphia or the Skillins of Boston (figures 25-28).

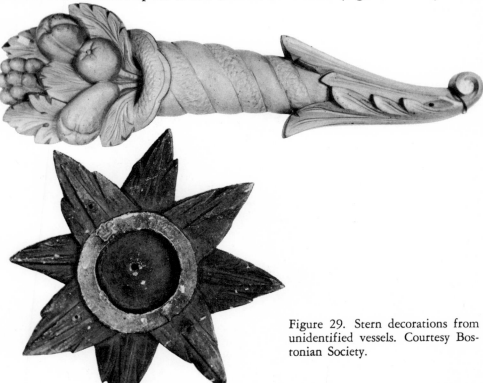

Figure 29. Stern decorations from unidentified vessels. Courtesy Bostonian Society.

McIntire was survived by one son, Samuel Field, who followed his father's trade. In 1815 he advertised that among other things he carved "Ship Heads, Festoons for Sterns", but when he died "of intemperance" in 1819 his estate shows he had a small business indeed. A first cousin, Joseph, at his death in 1852 left behind a considerable stock of carved work "finished and unfinished" including "Billet Heads; Stern Ornaments; carved eagles . .". None of the carvings or the designs by either man are known to exist.

Relatively, evidence concerning stern carvings of the Revolutionary period is more complete than it is for figureheads, for even though the bow decorations might be entirely omitted from Admiralty plans and from the two known American draughts, nearly all of them include at least the shape of the transom and galleries if not the full details of the design.[35] But it is very obvious from a comparison with British designs that no change had taken place in American carver's shops. Except for some simplification on this side of the Atlantic the designs are practically the same (figures 16-19).

Figure 30. Stern decoration from unidentified vessel, attributed to Simeon Skillin. Courtesy Peabody Museum of Salem.

III

Frigates and Packets

THE END of the War of Independence meant much more to the States than mere political separation from the Motherland. Freed from the maternalistic laws and traditions, native craftsmen began to be influenced by other European nations, France particularly. And more important they began to use their ingenuity to create styles and patterns of their own.

In shipcarving one craftsman, William Rush, seems to have felt the new freedom from English influence at once. His work as a shipcarver quickly spread the length of the Atlantic coast, teaching new forms and methods to the craftsmen of New Hampshire, Connecticut, Massachusetts and New York, as well as to those of South Carolina, Virginia and Maryland. Within a decade after the Revolution he gave the United States native shipcarvings the equal of any in the Old World, and ushered in what was certainly the grand period of American marine decorations.

Rush was born in Philadelphia July 4, 1756, the son of a local shipwright.[1] As a young boy he showed a decided interest in his father's trade and it is said he spent much of his time making models and sketches of the shipping he saw on the Delaware River. When about fifteen, he was apprenticed to Edward Cutbush, an English trained shipcarver who worked in Philadelphia.[2] Rush proved so apt a pupil that within three years his work was pronounced superior to that of his master.[3] Before his term of training could be completed, however, the colonies were at war with the Mother Country, and when the Howes descended on Philadelphia in 1777, Rush entered the Philadelphia Militia as an ensign.[4] As soon as the British evacuated the city, Rush seems to have returned to his home and set himself up in business since in 1779 he billed one Captain McNaughton for the carvings on the privateer *Revolution*. By 1785 Rush was owner of a shop in the maritime tradesmen's center along the Delaware River.[5] The next year Rush was assessed £50 in the business tax list, showing that he was fairly well established as compared with his older competitors, William Lake, who had a shipcarving business worth for taxes £75, and Edward Cutbush, Rush's old master, £50, no more than his former pupil.

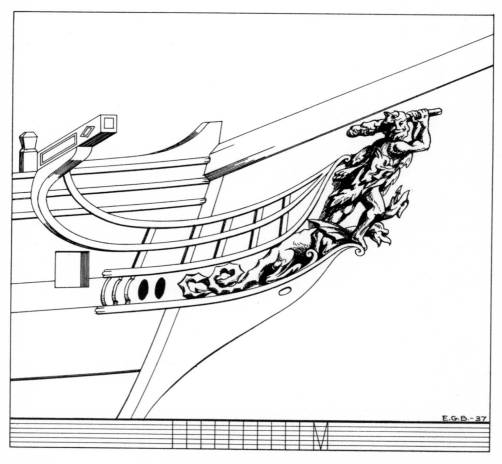

Figure 31. Figurehead of U.S. Frigate *Philadelphia,* 1799, by William Rush. From spar plan in Franklin Institute.

With the rapid rise in shipbuilding after the War — Philadelphia built forty vessels in 1783; thirteen ships, fifteen brigs, four schooners, and eight sloops — the local shipcarvers were busy.[6] But Rush was not

content to follow the old styles. Down at Joshua Humphreys' shipyard he had seen two French frigates, *La Danae* and *La Gloria,* repair-
ing.[7] In the heads of these two vessels Rush found the thing he was
seeking, something new to him and to all American carvers, figures
which seemed to be alive, figures in motion: not stiff, mechanical wood-
en images that looked like the queer gods that slave ships brought in
from Africa along with their cargoes of black ivory. France, during
the time of Colbert had organized a school under distinguished artists
for training shipcarvers. Their decorations for almost a hundred years
had been real works of art, figures that appeared to walk ahead of the
graceful hulls as if leading them onward.

These heads had an immediate effect on Rush and through him on
the other American carvers. The head of the ship *Washington* showed
the influence at once: "a figure of General Washington as large as life
. . . exhibiting a capital likeness . . . in full uniform as commander in
chief, pointing with his finger at some distant object and holding a
perspective glass grasped in his left hand". It was reported that on the
arrival of the vessel in the port of London the figurehead caused no
small sensation there "by the perfection manifest in all its parts and
proportions".[8] Another head by Rush, an "Indian trader", for the ship
William Penn likewise caused a commotion along the London docks,
when Captain James Josiah brought the ship up the Thames. "Carvers there would come in boats and lay near the ship and sketch the designs from it. They even came to take casts of plaster of Paris from the
head".[9] A third, a "River God" for the ship *Ganges* created a similar
sensation at Calcutta: "the Hindus came off in numerous boats to pay
their admiration and perhaps reverence".[10] Orders for figureheads
like these poured into Philadelphia shipcarvers. The sloop *Sally* cleared
on June 19, 1784 for Virginia carrying in her hold "1 Ships Head"; on
October 23 the sloop *Dispatch* sailed down the Delaware with one under her hatch; the New York packet on April 29, 1785 had one con-
signed to a New York shipbuilder.[11] The New Bedford whaler *Rebecca*
was launched in 1785 with a Philadelphia carved head on her bows.[12]
A commission for two heads for vessels building in London came to
Rush through the mercantile house of Nicklin and Griffith.[13] For
the Dey of Algiers he did "2 Lyons, very airy &c different attitudes,
one tearing a Fox to pieces, the other destroying a Tiger or Lioness,

Figure 32. Taffrail carving recovered from hull of Frigate *Philadelphia*. Courtesy U.S. Naval Academy.

Painted to the Life".[14]   And to crown all, when the United States decided to build a navy in 1794, Rush was commissioned to design all the
heads for the six frigates, four of which he carved himself.[15]   In these
designs Rush gave the country the first "group head".   That is, a head
composed of more than one figure, all of an allegorical nature to sym-
bolize what the carver considered the true import of the name of the
vessel.   Let Rush describe one of these:

> The genius of the UNITED STATES: she is crest with a Constellation her
> hair and drapery flowing. Suspended to the ringlets of hair which fall or
> wave over her Breast and reclining in her bosom is the portrait of her
> favorite son, George Washington President of United States; her waist
> bound with a Civic Band. In her right hand which is advanced she holds
> a spear suspended to which is a belt of Wampum containing the Emblems
> of Peace and War.   On her left side is a tablet which supports three large
> columns which relate to three Branches of Government; the Scale, emblam-
> atic of Justice, blended with them. The Left Hand suspends the Constitution
> over the book, &c. on the Tablet; the Eagle with his wings half extended,
> with the Escutcheon &c. of the Arms of the United States on the Right,
> designated the figure. The attributes, Commerce and Agriculture, and
> a modest position of the Arts and Sciences.[16]

This figurehead for the frigate *United States* has not been preserved, but the design of that for the frigate *Philadelphia*, 1799, has been.
It illustrates Rush's method of blending the designs of the trailboards
and the figurehead itself into an harmonious group — Hercules slaying
the seven-headed Hydra (figure 31).[17]

Traditionally the moving, lifelike figures and the group head were
not Rush's only contribution to our shipcarving.   In the early 1790's
at the request of Stephen Girard he began a series of portrait busts of
the great French philosophers, Rousseau, Montesquieu, etc., which were
fixed to the bows of vessels bearing those names.[18]   These, it was once
thought, were the first busts used in this country, but this is not correct.
A bust figurehead is depicted on a Marblehead vessel drawn by Ashley
Bowen in 1769.

In addition to his own work with the chisel, the training given to
apprentices helped spread Rush's ideas of design along the seaboard. One
of them, John Brown, went to Baltimore to work, executing among
others, heads for the sloops of war *Maryland* and *Patapsco*.   Another,
Daniel N. Train, moved to New York in 1799, doing the carved work
for the frigates *Adams*[19] and *Trumbull,* and probably that for the *New
York, President,* and *General Greene.*[20]   Rush himself sent the finished

VIRTUE

Figure 33. Figurehead by William Rush. Courtesy Masonic
Temple, Philadelphia.

heads for the *Chesapeake* to Norfolk, Virginia;[21] for the *John Adams* to Charleston, South Carolina;[22] for the *Congress* to Portsmouth, New Hampshire;[23] and for the *Constellation* to Baltimore, Maryland.[24] At the same time his designs for the *Constitution* were executed by John Skillin at Boston.[25] It is interesting to note that even at this early period in the history of our naval construction, the Secretary of the Navy was making the first of many efforts to discourage the use of figureheads. Writing in 1798, the Secretary said, "Heads are not useful and I believe injure a ship — If we must preserve an useless ornament . . . they aught not to be expensive". Obviously no attention was paid to his thoughts on the subject.[26]

Few of Rush's heads have survived the years. Figure 33 shows one of his early full length heads and figure 34 one of his busts. The bust was cut in 1815 for the ship of the line *Franklin*. It shows clearly the influence the great French sculptor Houdon had on Rush's portrait

Figure 34. Bust by William Rush for U.S.S. *Franklin,* 1815. Courtesy U.S. Naval Academy.

busts. The full length figure, now in the museum of the Masonic Temple in Philadelphia, was apparently never fixed on a vessel, which accounts for its perfect condition. One of the heads in The Mariners' Museum Collection, acquired in England but unknown as to vessel or carver, is so much like the Masonic Temple figure that it might be called an "identical twin sister". The facial features, the arrangement of the draperies, the treatment of the hair, the details of costume, all exactly follow each other. Perhaps one of the heads carved by Rush on the London order of Messrs. Nicklin and Griffith has come home. Every element in the extraordinarily fine figurehead of the Indian girl, called Pocahontas, at The Kendall Whaling Museum proclaims it to be Rush's work. The same may be said for the two quarter figures owned by the State Street Bank and Trust Company. Obviously all three are from the same vessel the identity of which is unknown. (frontispiece and figure 35).

When acquired by the Kendall Whaling Museum the figure of Pocahontas was thick with so many coats of paint the details of the carving were filled and therefore lost. From an outer bronze coat down to bare wood the paint was carefully removed and the color above the priming coat was replaced by Mrs. Kendall. The result gives a very close approximation of what the original was like when first the figure left the carver.

Rush's mastery of his material and his chisel, his skill at handling draperies, and his artistry in giving life to his work is fully shown in these surviving figureheads. If there is any doubt of his exact knowledge of the first requirement of a sculptor, anatomy, one has only to point to several sectional models of various parts of the human body which Rush made for the Medical School of the University of Pennsylvania. So exact are they that even today, over one hundred years after the carver's death, they are still in use. In addition, it is known that Rush studied assiduously the plates of Greek and Roman sculpture contained in Rees' *Encyclopedia* and in *The Artists Repository*. Rush died in 1833, but one of his sons, John, continued to follow the craft, although with little of his father's skill or inspiration.[27]

While William Rush might well be considered the springhead from which flowed the new conceptions and types of shipcarving, there were many craftsmen other than his apprentices who should be called

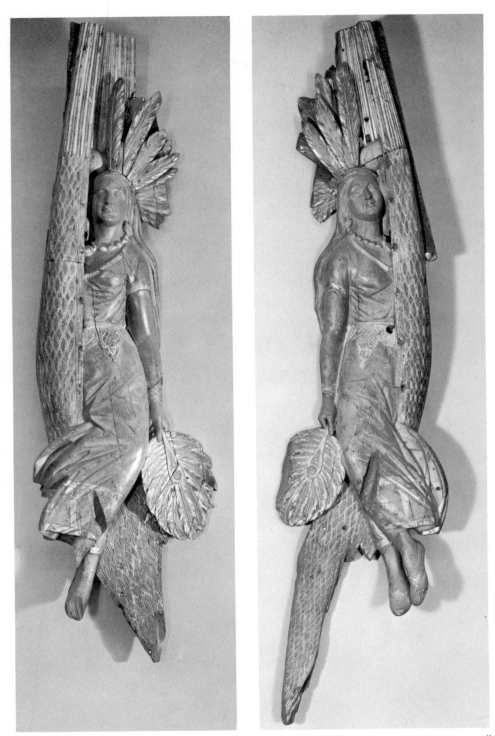

Figure 35. Stern carvings from unidentified vessel, probably the same as "Pocahontas" in frontispiece. Courtesy State Street Bank and Trust Co.

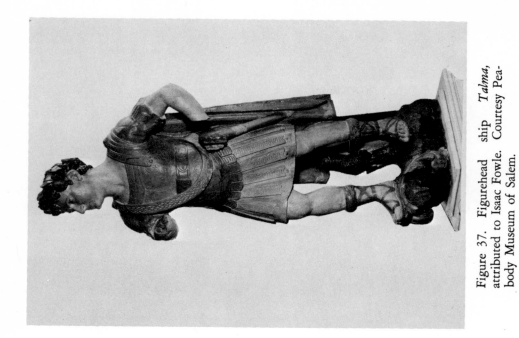

Figure 37. Figurehead ship *Talma*, attributed to Isaac Fowle. Courtesy Peabody Museum of Salem.

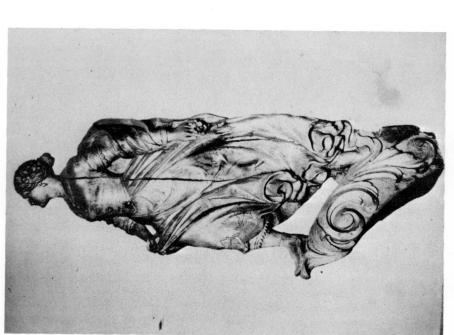

Figure 36. Figurehead by Isaac Fowle. Courtesy Bostonian Society.

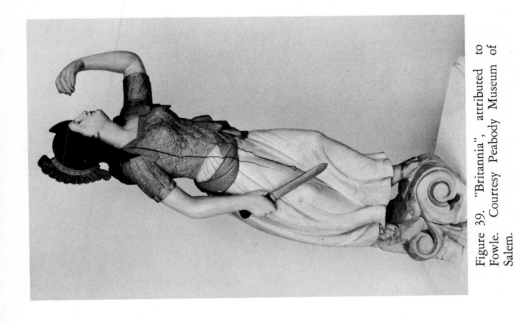

Figure 39. "Britannia", attributed to Fowle. Courtesy Peabody Museum of Salem.

Figure 38. Figurehead ship *Talma* [2nd]. Courtesy Century Club.

first rate, even if not Rush's equal. One of these was Isaac Fowle of Boston, who began business in 1807, possibly after serving an apprenticeship under the Skillins to whom the Fowles were related, or possibly under Edmund Raymond with whom Isaac formed a partnership. The firm lasted six years, until 1813, when Fowle went into business on his own account. During the next nineteen years Isaac Fowle built up a large business and was so well known that when he died or retired in 1832, his son John D. to capitalize the good-will organized a partnership, Isaac Fowle & Co. He was joined in 1836, by his brother, William H., and by one of Isaac's old apprentices, Spencer Beatty. When the latter died in 1853, a new partnership, J. D. & W. H. Fowle, was formed. That lasted until 1862 when William died. John continued the trade until 1869. Then after sixty years of continued shipcarving, the last of the Fowles died.[28]

Literally hundreds of figures must have passed through the doors of their shops in that time, but only two identified pieces have come down to us, one a head which for some reason was never fixed to a vessel. It is a full length figure of a woman, beautifully executed, with finely carved features and well handled drapes (figure 36). The pose has grace and strength of character. In fact, one can be critical only of the proportions of the lady's legs. This figure was done by Isaac Fowle himself about 1820. It is now preserved in the Old State House, Boston. The second, one of the *Constitution*'s Andrew Jackson heads, now at the Naval Academy, is a product of the Fowle shop. Another head, said to be from the packet *Lancashire*, 1835, certainly has all the earmarks of being by the same hand, and quite possibly may be another piece of Fowle workmanship. And on stylistic grounds the figurehead of the *Talma* and that of the armored woman, both at the Peabody Museum, could be attributed to the Fowle shop (figures 37-39).[29]

During Fowle's term of apprenticeship — even as early as 1781 — one development in the mechanics of ship decoration, purely local and apparently short lived, was to be found in Boston. There was so much work to be done for scores of new vessels being built that Boston's two or three carvers had every minute of their working time filled executing heads, quarter galleries, badges, and stern decorations. They had no time to do as carvers in other cities did: fix their own work to the vessels. Therefore Boston carvers turned their finished pieces over to specialized tradesmen known as "head builders". These men put the pieces on the hulls. Thus after the Skillins executed the carvings for the *Grand Turk*, the pieces were put into the hands of Joseph Robertson, "head builder". He took the forty-three odd pieces including the head, the rails, brackets, etc. to Enos Briggs' yard in Salem and assembled them on "Mr. Derby's great vessel". Similarly John Richardson did the same job for the Derby owned ship *Martha*. A bill which illustrates the functions of the head builder has been preserved in the Essex Institute, Ward Papers:

Mr. Ward to Thomas Richardson, Dr.,
for Building a head for the Brigg Tiger   9/6/9
for Fitting the Quarter pease and Tafreil   2/13/3
for Fitting Badges and nailing on   2/13/3
Boston August 9th 1781   14/13/3

The profession grew to such an extent that by 1796 the Boston *Directory* listed almost as many head builders as carvers.[30]

If Fowle's fine figureheads have disappeared and his work has been forgotten by his townsmen, one shipcarver at least has a lasting memorial that Bostonians can hardly neglect. High over their heads, stands the Bunker Hill Monument, designed by an itinerant shipcarver, Solomon Willard. He was born in 1783 at Petersham, Massachusetts, the son of a carpenter. As a boy Solomon worked in his father's shop until 1804 when he went to Boston to seek a job better than that of a country carpenter. While working at his trade, he studied wood carving, drawing, and anatomy. In 1813 he did his first job as a shipcarver. The next year he did "considerable carving, for parties in Providence and later went south to Virginia, Baltimore, Pennsylvania, and New York". While in Philadelphia, he met William Rush and on one occasion sketched work done by the master. In January 1816 Willard executed the bust figurehead for the seventy-four gun ship *Washington*, building at Portsmouth, New Hampshire (figure 40). In the head of this ship Willard followed the design in which the billet swept up over the top of the bust in such a manner that the figure appeared to be placed in a niche. This style, never widely used, accounts for the reduced size of the bust as compared to the eight or ten foot ones used on the other vessels of the same class. It is now preserved at the United States Naval Academy, although when photographed mislabeled *Potomac*. In 1817 Willard

Figure 40. Bust by Solomon Willard for U.S.S. *Washington*, 1817. Courtesy U.S. Naval Academy.

again went south and spent several months near Baltimore. After this trip he seems to have given up shipcarving and devoted himself entirely to stone work. He died, without descendants, in 1861.[31]

Another carver of the period, Laban S. Beecher of Boston, is remembered certainly not for the excellence of his best known work, the first Andrew Jackson figurehead, executed in 1834 for the frigate *Con-stitution*, but for the historic dispute that surrounded it. This head, now owned by the Seawanhaka Yacht Club and exhibited at the Marine Room, Museum of the City of New York, is by no means a masterpiece of design or workmanship. Quite possibly Beecher may have given play

Alabama. 74.

Figure 41. Design by Laban S. Beecher for U.S.S. *Alabama.* Courtesy U.S. Navy Department.

to a satirical sense of humor since two of his designs, heads for the ship of the line *Alabama* (figure 41) and the frigate *Santee*, both built at Portsmouth, are excellent.[32]

If traditional accounts of his work could be trusted, Joseph True of Salem was not only the artistic successor of Samuel McIntire but also one of the outstanding shipcarvers of his time. He was born in Chichester, New Hampshire August 1, 1785, and moved to Salem, Massachusetts about 1809. There is no evidence concerning his education or professional training. He worked in Salem until 1858 when he moved to Peoria, Illinois where he died in 1873.[33] His is one of the very few carver's account books which has been preserved, but even this is not complete.[34] The book, mixed in with hundreds of charges for cabinet carving between the years 1811 and 1856, includes only fourteen charges for ship work. The most important of these is ". . . twenty-four Ornaments for twenty-four Pillaster at $1.00 each" on November 6, 1816 for George Crowninshield's yacht *Cleopatra's Barge*. Typical others are: "To Carving Head for Schr [*Humming Bird*] $6.00." "To Carving three Ornaments for Stern & One Star Orn[ament] $6.00"; for George Turner's pilot boat "To Carving Head . . . $4.00"; Mr. Benjamin Webb's bark "A Head" $3.00; the brig *Mary Wilkins* two ornaments for cat heads fifty cents each; the brig *M. Shepard*, a carved quarter board, $3.00. Certainly none of these are large commissions with bills comparable to the several hundred dollar charges being made by other carvers at the same time. On the other hand, either True had another ledger or like many persons he failed to make entries for all the work he did. For instance in 1826 True carved the very handsome eagle for the Salem Custom House (it is still in its original position). His bill, $50.00, exists, but there is no book charge.[35] The Salem *Register* July 4, 1831, describing the launch of the ship *Eclipse* reported, "We were particularly struck with the carved work, executed by Joseph True . . . Her bow is adorned with the head of a Chinese emperor . . . on her stern are two beautiful female figures in white, one of them holding in her hand a representation of the Eclipse of the sun. . ." Another resident of Salem recalled the stern carvings of the ship *Crusoe*, built at Salem in 1828. ". . . Mr True . . . exhibited the sections of his elaborate stern piece, . . . covering the entire width, on which were truthfully and artistically represented Robinson himself, Friday, the goats, huts, trees and foreground, gilded and decorated [painted] in Mr. Shaw's inimitable Style, together with the figurehead equally skillful in carving and gilding . . ."[36] Since none of these important commissions are charged in the account book obviously our knowledge of his work is fragmentary. None of True's ship work has apparently been preserved, nor have any of his drawings, therefore it is necessary to fall back on other carved work to estimate his skill and here we run into contradictions. True's Custom House eagle is far superior to any existing McIntire eagle. McIntire and True each carved a head and a pair of hands for the two figures of Mandarins owned by the East India Marine Society. True's Chinese looks like a scarecrow; McIntire's Yamqua could easily be mistaken for a living person. With such contradictions True's place as a shipcarver must be left until more evidence comes to light.

In New York, Simeon Skillin and Daniel N. Train were the leaders in the art. But when shipbuilding began to flourish, shortly after 1800, one of the best shipcarvers was Jeremiah Dodge who set up in business about 1804. Like many other shipcarvers Dodge was the son of a shipwright. During his long career, he had several partnership connections: Skillin & Dodge, 1804-06; Dodge & Sharpe, 1815-21; and Jeremiah Dodge & Son, 1833-39. After the death of the father, the son, Charles J. Dodge, continued the business, until 1858, either as an individual or as a partner (1843-47) of Jacob S. Anderson.[37] The face carved by the Dodges for the *Constitution* is one of two pieces of their known work. The other piece is the Hercules cut for the ship of the line *Ohio* by Dodge & Sharpe in 1820 (figure 42). It is a splendid piece of carving, exhibiting the best class of work fitted to our naval vessels between 1815 and 1860. Another of the same type, equally as good was the head of the *Columbus,* copied by William Rush from the statue in the Cathedral at Havana. This style of heroic bust figurehead was the favorite, almost the official type used on naval vessels after 1815. Captain John Smith's bust graced the bow of the *Potomac;* that of Alexander the Great, the second *Macedonian;* Sir Walter Raleigh's head and chest were worn by the *North Carolina;* Captain Charles Stewart's, by the second *Cyane.*

Similarly the bust had its effects on merchant vessels and from the middle of the 1820's until the middle of the 1850's, it was very popular on the smaller merchant ships. There were several reasons for

Figure 43. Bust from ship *St. Paul*, 1833. Courtesy Ross Whittier, Esqr.

Figure 42. Bust by Dodge & Sharpe from U.S.S. *Ohio.* Photo in Peabody Museum of Salem.

this. Busts were less expensive. They required considerably less skill in execution. They were less susceptible to damage; and a life-sized bust was in proportion to the vessel where a full length figure would have been not only unbecoming in size but also too heavy for the head structure. A number of these heads have been preserved. The *Falconer* in the Rat's Club in Boston; the *Solomon Piper* head at the Peabody Museum; the *Daniel Webster* at The Mariner's Museum; and one unidentified at the Bourne Museum are examples. Certainly one of the most

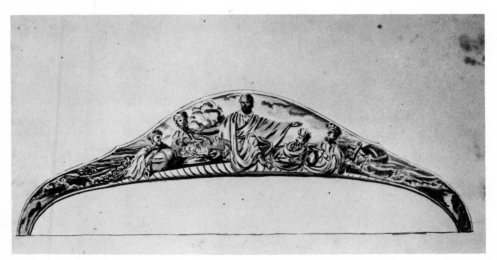

Figure 44. Design for stern ship *St. Paul*, 1833. Courtesy Peabody Museum of Salem.

Figure 45. Dragon knee-type figurehead. Courtesy Mariners' Museum.

handsome busts which has been preserved is that from the ship *Saint Paul* (figure 43) built at Boston in 1833 presumably by Gad Leavitt, who signed the master carpenter's certificate. A few years later she was sold to Stephen C. Phillips and others of Salem and during an extensive repair at Salem in 1849, the head was removed and mounted on a Phillips wharf warehouse.[38] A portrait of the ship *Saint Paul* in the Peabody Museum shows the bust quite clearly. Instead of the present solid white color, the hair and beard are brown and the edges of the toga are light blue. The design of the stern carving is in the Peabody Museum (figure 44). Since this drawing came from the collection gathered by Warren Hastings in Boston it is reasonable to believe the head came from one of Hastings' carver predecessors, perhaps Beecher. The vessel was sold in the Philippines in 1851, after being badly damaged there, consequently the whereabouts of the stern decorations is not known.

During the entire period of William Rush's career and for about fifteen years afterward, vessel's bows, merchant as well as naval, all followed the style set by the frigates of the late eighteenth century; heavily kneed, with full head rails, trailboards and brackets. The figures themselves instead of being applied in high relief on the knee were, of

Figure 46. Design for figurehead ship *King Philip,* 1854. Courtesy Peabody Museum of Salem.

course, modeled in full round, usually standing on a strong scroll which capped the top of the knee. No portion of the knee extended up through the figure thereby separating the right leg from the left. To use a carver's term, they were "cut clear and through". The head rails swept up to a scroll of their own, all joining at the shoulders of the figurehead to give it additional support. In the true bust heads, a bracket, almost a shelf, was formed on the top of the knee to serve as a base for the figure. On this the bust was fastened with the rails coming in between the shoulders to give strength. In those busts which were what might be called three-quarter figures, the lower portion was cut in such a manner that it fitted exactly to the curve of the head knee and was bolted directly to it. The head of the McKay packet *Jenny Lind* (figure 51), launched at Boston in 1848, was one of this type. The walking design cut clear and through did not in every instance supplant the older "straddle head" and it is very probable a few straddle heads were carved as late as 1810 or 1815.

For ships, barks, and ordinary schooners the walking figureheads were the same in basic design with variations only in size and proportions to fit the hull. But for the racehorse of the seas, the Baltimore Flyer, another type was evolved. Early in their development they had become the pilot boats, the privateers, the smugglers and slavers, craft from whom the utmost speed was required. All non-essentials such as heavy heads with their rails and brackets, trailboards, quarter galleries and fancy stern decorations were stripped from their hulls. Occasionally one piece was left out over the stem, a strong but light knee to which the bowsprit could be gammoned. Forward of its lashing was a nude timber end. That quickly became a bit of carved work, usually nothing more than a tiny head, perhaps human, perhaps animal. Its descendants can be seen on the craft of the Chesapeake today, out at the end of the long head of the bugeyes, skipjacks, and bay schooners. So far as is known only one of the early heads of this type remains (figure 45). Of it unfortunately nothing is known, and the sole means of identifying it lies in the plans of some of the Baltimore Flyers of the 1800-25 period in which similar gammon knees are shown. Carved timbers of this type were in use in 1789, since Samuel McIntire of Salem in that year billed Elias Derby for £1.1.0. "By Carv'g a knee for Schooner *Nancy*".[39]

Figure 47. Archboard from unidentified ship. Courtesy Kendall Whaling Museum.

Figure 48. Design for stern of unidentified vessel. Courtesy Peabody Museum of Salem.

Full figure or bust, these were the types of heads used during the entire period of the frigate-built packet ships which brought to the United States the vast hordes of emigrants from Ireland, England and the Continent. But whichever type graced the bow, just as the "lyon", the horse, and the classical figures were the principal motifs in earlier years, so now a comparatively few basic designs were used. One of them, a favorite in New England, was the Indian chief (figure 46). The Revenue Cutter *Massachusetts*, 1791, the frigate *Essex*, 1799, and the ship *Boston*, a Nor'west man of 1803, each carried one; so did the Crowninshield privateer *America*, 1812, the work of Edward Dorr, Retire Becket's head builder. William Rush carved several from the Indian trader for the *William Penn* in the 1790's to the Cope packet *Algonquin*, 1824, the latter "An Indian Chief in a beaver robe in the attitude of declaiming". A contemporary described some of the redmen in these words:

> Placing him [the Indian] in exact position either as drawing his arrow to the head at the supposed bounding deer; flourishing his tomahawk with fatal aim; or else in attitude of solemn thought with his arms folded within his blankets drawn closely around him, and showing exactly the contour of his brawny person and limbs. The frontlet of destruction fastened upon his forehead and pinioned behind with the eagle's plume. The head cloasly shaved, leaving only the single tuft of black hair . . . his faithful dog, crouching at his heels. Each figure head was so admirably brought out from its original block of wood and coloured to the life under the directions from the sculptor that the beholder would be almost ready to imagine he hears the distant savage yell.[40]

Another favorite motif was the portrait type, perhaps the owner's wife or daughter, wasp-waisted with billowing bosom, full wide skirts, white stockings, and dainty black pumps. Or in the case of vessels of the Dramatic Line of Liverpool packets, portraits of their namesakes: Siddons, Shakespeare, Garrick, etc. One of these heads, badly worn by time and the elements is to be seen in the Museum at Mystic Seaport. It is the bust carried by the *Shakespeare*, cut by John Frazier of New York in 1835. Or perhaps a famous person of the day, such as Daniel Webster, whose figure graced the bows of the packet of that name.

A description of one of the vessels built towards the end of the period gives clearly the sort of figureheads found during the entire time and the profuseness of the carved work. Philip Hone, the New York

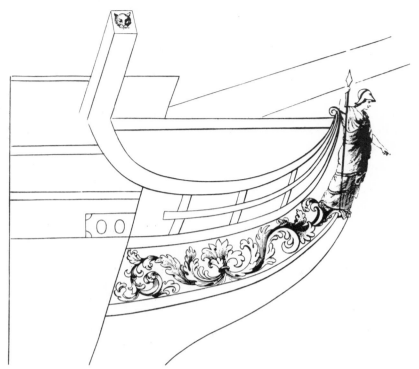

Figure 49.   Design for figurehead of unidentified Philadelphia packet ship.
From L. McKay: *Practical Shipbuilder*.

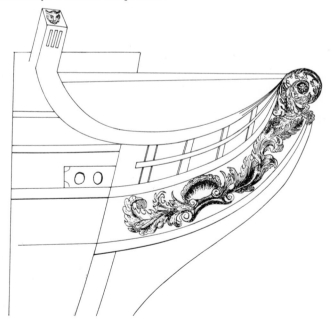

Figure 50.   Billet head and trailboard designed by L. McKay.   From L.
McKay;   Practical Shipbuilder.

Figure 51. Figurehead ship *Jenny Lind*. Courtesy Mariners'
Museum.

diarist, on December 6, 1841, went to see the launching of the Havre packet *Saint Nicholas*. Of the carvings he wrote:

> The ship bears on her bow a full-length figure of the patron saint, in full cannonicals and her stern is ornamented with a representation of the same worthy in his better-remembered capacity of the friend and benefactor of our early days. He is represented here entering a chimney loaded with his annual gifts for 'good children' which he is supposed to have brought from Holland via his ariel railroad, in less time than is required in these boasted times of rapid locomotion to get up the steam of the *Great Western*, and in another portion of the same carving we see the kind-hearted saint filling the stockings with his farfetched treasures . . . The latter scene is copied from Weir's admirable picture on this subject.[41]

This vessel represented one of the last of the frigate-built packets to be laid down. With that class (figure 49) passed the heavy knee head, the rails and brackets, and, usually the trailboards; with it passed the quarter galleries, the square wide two-decked transom with arch board and stern windows, all of which gave to the shipcarver a broad surface for the display of his art. The packet had provided his last chance for lavish ornament; slowly but with certainty the demand for speed in ships was sweeping towards a culmination which would do away with most of the shipcarver's work.

IV
Clippers

IN THE middle of the nineteenth century, as the result of a long series of events in the marine world, the Clipper Ship arrived. With it came new designs in figureheads. John W. Griffiths, who had so much to do with the development of the Clipper, writing in 1850 said, "There is a certain fitness about the head of a ship which at once stamps an impression on the mind in relation to the entire ship, and why? We say that the head of a ship is like a portrait, we look at the physiognomy of the man and judge his intellectual endowments — of his internal and external qualities; so with a ship".[1]

The old packets with their sweeping rails, brackets, and heavy figurehead, their rows of stern windows all gave an impression of stateliness, steadiness and regularity. But who cared for that when gold lay around the Horn for the first comer to pick up? Speed was the word. And psychologically to gain the carrying trade the whole ship had to convey that thought. Hence with the clippers almost every element of design was bent to that one prime essential.

Therefore just as the Baltimore Flyers of an earlier date had been divested of practically all their decorations so in their younger cousins, the clippers, all unnecessary weights were discarded. Stripped as bare as Grecian athletes they dashed from port to port as fast as wind and man power would allow. The only exceptions to their nudity lay in a light carved piece on the stern and a figurehead. But in both, changes in design and method of mounting were made to assure minimum weight.

William H. Webb of New York, one of the foremost builders, quickly did away with the full carved head on his vessels, and his work represented the course chosen by some builders. His *Challenge*, built in 1851, carried an eagle on her stem with carved cat heads.[2] The *Invincible* built the same year had only a "Liberty Cap", a bit of carving hardly larger than the original head covering.[3] He built no clippers in

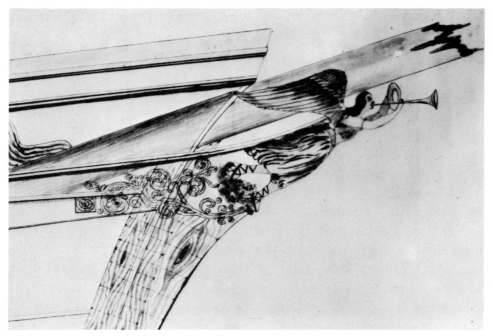

Figure 52. Design for figurehead *Chariot of Fame,* built by D. McKay. Courtesy Peabody Museum of Salem.

1852, but the next year his *Flyaway* discarded the head," the stem elongating to the bowsprit, there being a gigantic pair of spread wings, indicating flight over the waves".[4] The *Young America,* 1853, perhaps Webb's best known vessel, had only a very simple billet head.[5] Webb seems to have used Charles McColley for many of his pieces of carved work but the expenditures for them are all comparatively small, indicating almost an aversion for decoration, except when dealing with a government such as Italy or Russia.

Not all builders followed Webb's extreme examples; most of them, indeed, made use of one of three forms of heads.

First of all, the design of the head knee was altered. The type found on the old packets — the curves, low to the water carrying the figure in an almost vertical position—had to have the support of cheek knees, rails, etc. Commenting on this type — "The English Clipper or snipe bow", as it was then called—one critic said, "Of all bows this is the most objectionable; its great, useless, overhanging weight, having a tendency to weaken the ship, and there is danger in heavy weather of spooning up an extra quantity of sea water and flooding the decks".[6] So about 1845, when the clipper packets began to be built, the designers raised the knee higher from the water and elongated it. Being clear of the seas the rails and cheek knees were no longer necessary. There was, of course,

Figure 53. Daguerreotype of clipper *Seamans Bride*, 1851. Courtesy Maryland Historical Society.

no possible way of fastening the figure to this type of head in a vertical
position. Therefore it was placed on an inclined position along the
outer end and underside of the knee with a portion of the figure itself

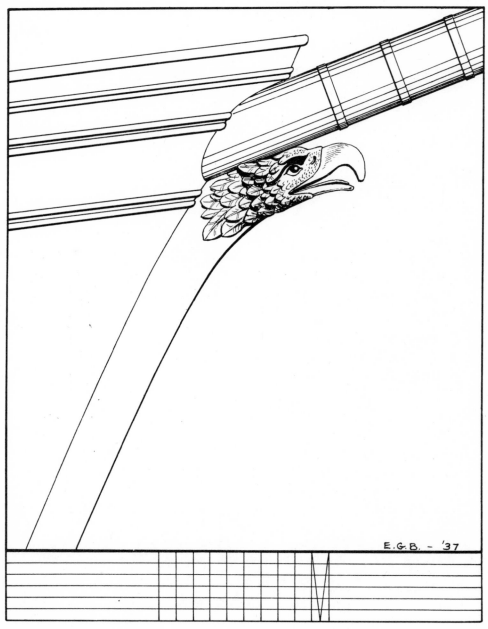

Figure 54. Figurehead clipper *Great Republic,* 1853. From plan of vessel.

cut away to fit the timbers which composed the knee structure. In other words, the figure straddled the knee. Not, however, as it had in the eighteenth century with the knee protruding between the legs of the figure, but with the back of the figure cut away, enfolding and covering the knee. These figures were still "cut clear and through" in the fullest meaning of the term, for their design was such that parts of the knee were hidden by portions of the figure, the body not the legs.

This type of figurehead carried down well towards the end of the century and is the one generally associated with the clipper ship in the term "clipper bow". A very few years after it had been worked out, a modification was devised in which the elongation of the knee under the bowsprit was eliminated and the head itself was fixed in place. Support for the figure was given by a timber, called a "lacing piece" bolted into the frames extending along the figure's upper side. The figurehead of the clipper *Chariot of Fame* built by Donald McKay at Boston in 1853 illustrates this type of head. Figure 52 is taken from the builder's longitudinal section plans.[7] Many of the clippers carried heads of this type for they were almost exactly suited to the designs of the sharp flaring bows. They had the required lightness of weight, and above all the pose of the figure itself, leaning sharply forward, gave the impression of speed "in relation to the entire ship". It had, in fact, but one fault; structural weakness in its manner of fastening, and many of the clippers' logs record that gales "carried away the figurehead".

Contemporary to this type of head was another which towards the end of the era appears to have been the favorite. In this the entire knee of the head was eliminated and the figure was fixed to the top of the cutwater itself. This type seems to have been first used on the clipper *Gazelle*, built at New York in 1850-51 by Webb. A description written at the time she was built says, "She has a very small and short cutwater, or head, totally different from the old style — which, on account of the great length, was very objectionable — and has but little ornamental carving. The cutwater is fitted or framed in the ship in so strong a manner that it will require an extraordinarily heavy sea to displace any portion of it".[8]

Contrast the bow of the clipper *Seamans Bride* built in Baltimore by the Bells in 1851, a good representative of the old style. The photograph, figure 53, taken just before she was launched shows the heavy head

Figure 55. Figurehead clipper *Great Republic*. Courtesy Mystic Seaport.

structure supported by cheek rails (though these are somewhat disguised by the naval woods) and a comparatively small figurehead. It is a graceful bow to be sure, but it contradicts the previous development around Baltimore on the fast vessels of smaller size wherein the bow had been stripped of all unnecessary weights. At the time of her launch it was reported, " . . . Her stem is ornamented with a gilt eagle with wings thrown back as though stooping for flight. The effect is improved by it being artistically placed in line with her stem, thereby obviating an ugly angle that sometimes detracts from similar ornaments". Of course the reporter's point of view was not exactly that of the camera's; he saw the head from broadside and the figure followed the curve of the knee without breaking the sweep. The carver was James Randolph of Baltimore who between 1850 and 1857 did the carvings for fifteen major vessels to say nothing of minor jobs. Perhaps the most unusual of Randolph's pieces was the head of the clipper *Canvas Back* which included an entire flock of that well-known Maryland duck in flight.[9] The figurehead of the *Great Republic* built by McKay in 1853, (figure 55) the same year as the *Chariot of Fame* represented another of the *Gazelle* type. It was a huge eagle's head with open beak and glaring eyes, the work of S. W. Gleason & Sons of Boston. A description of the ship written by a reporter who saw her launched said, "Such a bow for sharpness, beauty, and strength, has never before been produced in this coun-

Figure 56. Figurehead clipper *David Crockett* by Jacob Anderson. Courtesy San Francisco Chamber of Commerce.

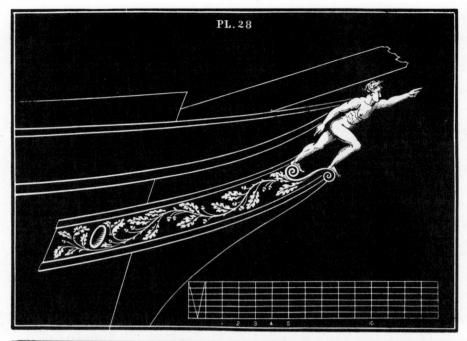

Figure 57. Figurehead designs by John W. Griffiths. From John W. Griffiths: *Marine and Naval Architecture.*

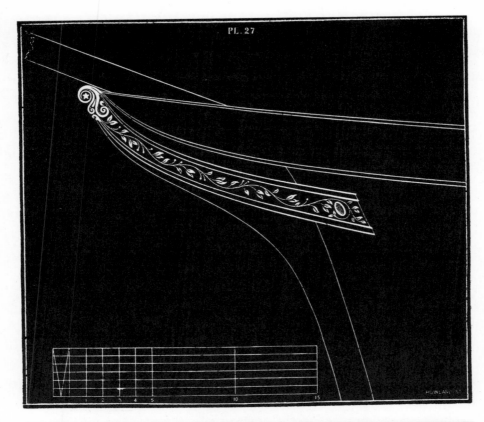

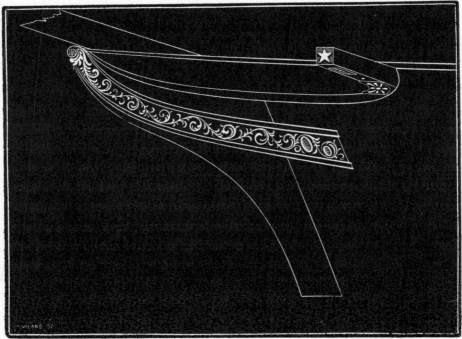

Figure 58.   Billet heads and trailboards by John W. Griffiths. From John W.
Griffiths: *Marine and Naval Architecture*.

try. Yet it is plain even to nakedness, having a national eagle represented as emerging from below the bowsprit as its only ornament".[10] The illustration of the manner of placement is taken from a contemporary copy of the longitudinal section plan (figure 54). The actual head is now preserved at Mystic Seaport, Connecticut.

Such were the designs of the figureheads used on the ships of the Clipper Era. What were the motifs most popular and who were the men who created the heads? Clippers were built from Maine to Florida, but the chief centers were New York City, Mystic, Boston, its vicinity, and Portsmouth. In these ports were found the shipcarvers most worthy of attention.

The motifs used were almost as widely assorted as the names of the vessels themselves. As usual with American craft, eagles were the prime favorite: on some the full bird with outstretched wings; on others simply the bird's head. McKay's *Bald Eagle,* Webb's *Challenge,* Curtis's *Competitor* were examples of the first; the *Great Republic* and the *Hurricane* among others of the second.[11] Other birds were used, a gilded pigeon on Hall, Snow & Co. of Bath's *Carrier Pigeon;*[12] or a fighting cock "with outstretched neck and head" on the *Game Cock* built by Hall of Boston.[13] A gilt race horse pranced at the bows of the *Racer.*[14] The *Charmer* from Jackman's Newburyport yard carried a "snake with the tongue hanging out of its mouth as if it had a drink of Cochituate water and did not like it".[15] Dragons of the Chinese variety were fixed on the bows of the *Sea Witch,* the *Tinqua,* the *Winged Racer,* and others.[16]

Handsome as these animals may have been the best of the heads were the human figures. For instance, the full length figure of David Crockett (figure 56), cut for the clipper of that name built at Mystic, by Greenman & Co. in 1853. This head, in splendid condition because it was never affixed to the vessel, was cut by Jacob Anderson of New York.[17] Just who he was or where he was trained is not known. He appears first in the New York City *Directory* of 1830-31 as "Jacob Anderson & Co". Two years later the "& Co." was dropped and he worked as an individual until 1843. Then he formed a partnership, Dodge & Anderson, with Charles J., son of the carver Jeremiah Dodge. This firm lasted until 1847 when Anderson was again working alone. He was joined in 1856 by his son John, with a title of "J. S. Anderson & Son". Two years later Jacob was dead, and, although his widow Jane attempted to carry on the business, the shop door was closed in 1860. It is to be hoped more of Jacob's work will be found for certainly he was one of the master shipcarvers of all time.[18]

Another shop whose work was of the first order was the firm of S. W. Gleason & Sons of Boston. The firm went through many changes of name during its long career. Founded in 1847 it flourished under that name until 1854 when one of the sons, William B., succeeded to the business. In 1863 the firm styled itself McIntyre & Gleason. Nine years later Herbert Gleason assumed the sole responsibility until 1878 when he joined with another Boston carver, E. Warren Hastings. This firm, Hastings & Gleason, lasted until 1896, when Mr. Hastings took down his sign. During the Clipper Era the Gleasons executed many heads for famous vessels; the eagle for the *Great Republic;* the bronzed merman blowing a conch shell for the *Sovereign of the Seas;* the "gilded staghound panting in the chase" for the *Staghound;* and other figures for the McKay-built fleet. One has been preserved, that of the *Great Republic* and another is attributed to Gleason, the *Minnehaha* at Williamsburg, Virginia.[19] Many of the designs of heads and sterns which passed through this firm are owned by the Peabody Museum in the Warren Hastings Collection.

A second Boston carver of the period, John W. Mason, attained considerable fame with his work. Born in Ireland on July 13, 1814, he moved to Boston when a young man and by 1838 had married and set up as a carver in Commercial Street. He was one of the best carvers of the packet period; one on whom McKay depended for the decorations of his earlier vessels, for instance the *Anglo-Saxon* (figure 59).[20] Many of his designs for carved work have been preserved, although few of the actual pieces remain. His best creation perhaps was the head for the clipper *Witch of the Wave,* built by George Raynes of Portsmouth, N.H. in 1851.[21] Because Duncan MacLean, the marine reporter of the Boston *Atlas* wrote such a complete account of all the vessel's carved work, the description is worth quoting in full.

> A female figure, beautiful as an houri, and placed to correspond with the spring of the bow ornaments her forward. The figure is represented in flowing vestments of white, fringed with gold; and she bears aloft a scarf, half unfurled by the breeze. From her pedestal descend branches of gold, which also encircle the hawsehole. Her name, in gilded letters, is on the monkey rail, close abaft the bowsprit; and on the end of each cathead is a

Figure 59. Design for figurehead ship *Anglo-Saxon* by John W. Mason. Courtesy Peabody Museum of Salem.

Figure 60. Figurehead design "Neptune" by John W. Mason. Courtesy Peabody Musem of Salem.

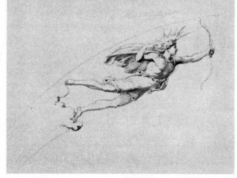

Figure 62. Design for figurehead ship *Morning Light* by John W. Mason. Courtesy Peabody Museum of Salem.

Figure 61. Figurehead design "Queen of Sheba" by John W. Mason. Courtesy Peabody Museum of Salem.

gilded head; but the most remarkable features of her ornamental work forward are her [the vessel's, not the figure's] eyes, one glowering from each
bow, as if scanning the foaming deep before. As she is planked up to the
bowsprit, without either head or trail boards, no matter how heavily she may
plunge, when she rises, like a duck, she can raise no water with her.

The elegant ease with which her bow is carried up, is continued in her
gradual sheer along the side, until it terminates in the stern, the outline of
which is perfectly oval. Her run is rounded, and the planking of the sides
and quarters is moulded to correspond. She has no apparent transom outside,
but the stern is at once formed from the rudder case, with a slight rake aft
as it rises. Upon it is a representation of her name, floating in a shell, with
an imp, on the larboard side, riding a dolphin, and on the opposite side
other members of the finny family sporting in the sea. Above these is her
name, in gilded letters, and below it her port of hail, with a star on each
side and a wreath of roses below, the whole enclosed in a gilded frame. The
principal figures are painted white, relieved with gilding on either side. No
pains have been spared to render the stern a perfect picture. Her name, in
gilded letters, is also placed on her bulwarks, between the main and mizen
rigging.

All of Mason's existing designs are in the Peabody Museum.

In Newburyport the two Wilson brothers, James W. and Albert
H., had almost a monopoly of the carvings done for the vessels locally
built. They were the sons of a shipcarver, Joseph W. Wilson, who had
come to Newburyport in 1798.[22] Their firm was organized in 1851
after the sons had served as apprentices and journeymen. None of their
work is definitely known to exist, but possibly the head (figure 64), now
in The Mariners' Museum, of the *Black Prince* built at Newburyport in
1854 should be credited to them. If so, then the magnificent figure over
the door of the Seamens Church Institute of New York is surely from
their shop (figure 65). Unquestionably both were cut by the same hand.

Figure 65. Unidentified figurehead. Courtesy Seaman's Church Institute, New York.

Figure 64. Figurehead *Black Prince*. Courtesy Mariners' Museum.

In design and workmanship the latter is one of the finest figureheads ever executed, well worthy to stand with the best work of William Rush, Isaac Fowle, or Jacob Anderson.[23]

Portsmouth, a prominent shipbuilding point from the earliest colonial days, had more than a small share in constructing clippers. Many of their heads were cut in Boston; since Portsmouth had at the time, but one local carver, Woodbury Gerrish. When he began to work and where he learned his trade is not known. Probably it was in Boston since he worked for a time in Charlestown, both privately and at the Navy Yard. Later he moved to Portsmouth where he worked until his death.

Figure 66. Bust from U.S.S. *Franklin* by Woodbury Gerrish, 1853. Courtesy U.S. Naval Asylum, Philadelphia.

One piece of his work is now preserved at the Naval Asylum, Philadelphia, a small bust cut for the ship of the line *Franklin* when she was razeed at Portsmouth in 1853 (figure 66). It is one of the few signed figureheads known. The piece is well cut, but it has none of the excellence of the Houdonesque portrait which Rush had cut for the same vessel in 1815. Most of Gerrish's work was done for the United States Navy, but he also carved for private customers and maintained a shop until the middle seventies.[24]

In Mystic, Connecticut, John Colby and James Campbell were working for the vessels built by Greenman and the Mallory yard. In Rockland, Maine, the birthplace of the *Red Jacket* and other fine ships Verill supplied many of the decorations. At Baltimore, in addition to James Randolph already mentioned, James Mullen (later Mullen and Van Wynen) and James Mullen of O were the principal carvers of the period. Mullen did the work for the *Rattler* and the *Spirit of the Time* both clippers; Randolph, the *Toothpick,* renamed *Kate Hooper,* the *Flying Childers, Canvas Back,* and *Seamans Bride;* and James Mullen of O the head of the clipper *Carrier Dove* which caused the marine reporter of the Baltimore *Sun* to remark "The figure-head and its attendant carvings do great credit to the artist. But, we had a notion to question the taste of the designer, who placed a half-clothed woman in the place that a Carrier Dove, a messenger of old . . . to Father Noah, should occupy. However, that is a mere matter of taste. We cannot call that woman a 'bird'."[25]

Good work these and other men did, but by the end of the decade the volume had materially diminished. In the naval service the same conditions prevailed. An economic depression had struck the land in 1857. Shipbuilding declined in volume to such an extent that many shipcarvers were driven into other trades. Then the War between the States broke out taking so many of the remaining carvers into the armed services that even vessels built for the navies were turned out virtually without decorations of any character. During the war years the craft was practically non-existant.

With the new models of clipper hulls came the round and eliptical sterns which gave very little chance for the carver to exhibit his skill. A comparatively small piece cut in low relief was usually all that the carver provided other than the letters spelling out the vessel's name

Figure 67. Design for figurehead ship *Empire State.* Courtesy Peabody Museum of Salem.

and hailing port. Of course, by now all vestige of the galleries and badges had disappeared completely.

How a shipbuilder or owner obtained a figurehead during the period is interesting. If he intended to patronize a local carver, a consultation between owner, builder and carver would settle the whole matter of size, motif, and cost. But if the owner was at some distance from either or both of the others, correspondence was involved. By good fortune some of this has survived. Richard H. Tucker of Wiscasset, Maine, was having Fernald & Pettigrew of Portsmouth, New Hampshire, build a ship. On their recommendation Tucker wrote John L. Cromwell of New York, carver, to give his "particular directions" for a "bust head, Taffrail or Sterns moulding". "Will you have the goodness to give me a scetch of the Stern Mouldings & design to correspond with her name. Also the design of the bust as regards costume & head dress, that I may suggest an alteration if necessary. The name I wish kept CONFIDENTIAL so that no one else shall assume it before I do". In fact, Tucker kept the name so confidential he did not even put it in the letter, but Cromwell

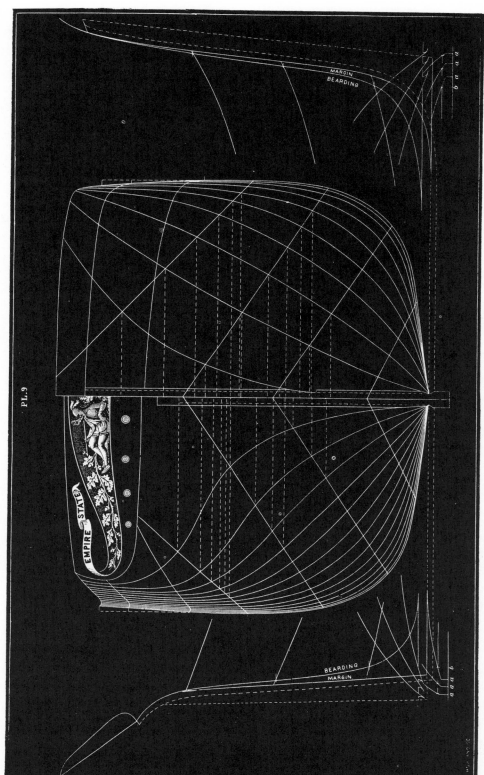

Figure 68. Design for stern ship *Empire State* by John W. Griffiths. From John W. Griffiths: *Marine and Naval Architecture*.

Figure 69. Figurehead from unidentified vessel. Courtesy Peabody Museum of Salem.

Figure 70. Stern eagle attributed to C. A. L. Sampson. Courtesy Peabody Museum of Salem.

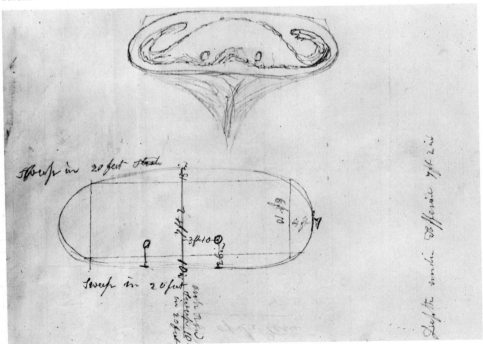

Figure 71. Preliminary sketch for stern decoration ship *Dashing Wave*. Courtesy Peabody Museum of Salem.

learned it by further correspondence and Tucker we hope got the sketch he wanted for a bust of *Samoset.* The drawing has not come to us so we can not see if the head dress was Sioux, Cherokee, or Abenaki.[26]

Another long range piece of designing took place for the ship *Empire State,* this time with Charles J. Dodge of New York. This design with specifications and dimensions went back to Portsmouth and we trust was used. It would have been a fine piece if the carving was up to the drawing (figure 67).[27]

A third letter provides further knowledge as to how the carver of the Clipper Era worked. On March 6, 1850, S. W. Gleason & Sons, Carvers, 82 Commercial Street, Boston wrote Fernald & Pettigrew.

Gentlemen

Your favor of the 5th inst is at hand together with the sketch of the head of the *Western World,* for which we are greatly obliged to you & which no doubt will be of some assistance to us in regard to thickness of cut water &c &c. You have sent us the rake of the stem & steve of bowsprit: if you will please let us know about the distance you want the upper-side of lower cheek from the underside of bowsprit on the line of the stem, & the distance you want the figure to set out on the line of the bowsprit, and the distance out on the bowsprit of the inner bobstay, we shall be able to furnish a draft on a scale to set the head by: or perhaps it would be better if you would lay the model on a sheet of paper & mark the line of the stem & the shear of the wale streak, this is necessary as the butt end of the lower-cheeck should start on a parallel line, & for billet heads generally starts from the same line but may be carried lower, where a greater distance is wanted for a figure. In answer to your question about the size of the figure we would say that we agree with you pretty much, that is to say, we think that the figure should look the size of life after it is on & would have to be in reality 3 or 5 in taller, the standard height among Artists is for a female 5 feet 3 in — suppose we make the figure 5 feet 6 in & the block or scroll as small as possible say 7 in — extreme length of whole 6 feet 1 inch; how will that do? We can furnish you with a beautiful stern piece of shell work similar to the one you saw us at work upon, & if you wish for extra work in the centre — figures or any thing of that kind, we can substitute them for a part of the shell work — unless you should, we shall go right at work upon the stern as soon as we get the dimensions. We have no doubt that you can have the figure before the first of July.[28]

V

The End of the Art

THE YEAR 1855 saw the peace time peak of American sailing ship construction—1781 vessels. From then on came a steady decline. In 1875, only 798 sailing vessels of all types and sizes were launched; ten years later, 533, and in 1895 only 397 left the stocks.[1]

To the shipcarver this trend meant extinction of his craft. Apprentices no longer sought to be indentured; the old familiar signs of the masters handed down through generations disappeared. That of Samuel L. Winsor "Ship Carving UpStairs" (figure 72) was first hung out over a Boston doorway in 1839, serving him until 1851; then doing duty for Messrs Stoddard & McLoughlin, who had moved to Boston from Maine; next for McIntyre & Gleason; next for their successor Herbert Gleason, and finally Hastings & Gleason until the death of the last partner, E. Warren Hastings in 1896.[2]

During the last period of the American sailing vessels no new ship designs brought forth any technical necessity for innovations in figurehead styles. The old forms of the clipper era, especially those springing direct from the cutwater were used exclusively. Even building metal vessels in the United States had no influence since the figureheads merely followed the designs already well developed in the British Isles for such vessels.

But these last years were not without examples to prove that skill with mallet and chisel still existed. Shipbuilding following the Civil War had shifted from the older centers at New York, Philadelphia, and Baltimore to be virtually a monopoly of Massachusetts and Maine. To these states, then, one must look for figureheads and their carvers.

Not that New York, Philadelphia, and other shipbuilding points entirely stopped supplying their vessels with heads. But with the decline of ship construction, carving in those places seems to have degenerated into a series of conventional designs. For instance, even as early as 1852

77

Figure 72. Shipcarver's shop sign. Courtesy Bostonian Society.

Samuel Hubbart of Baltimore had "Heads for Vessels of all sizes always on hand" and Charles McColley of New York advertised in 1868 "Carved Eagles and Billet Heads constantly on hand" to furnish the ordinary run of vessels with only exceptionally well finished craft having special attention in individual designs.[3]   In Boston, Herbert Gleason, the son of McKay's carver, executed the magnificent head for McKay's last famous clipper, the *Glory of the Seas* (figure 73).   This figure, now in an honored position at India House, New York, is almost the swan song of the craft.   Never after it was so much beauty of design, so much skill and freedom of execution to be brought together. Gleason with his partner, Warren Hastings, and Joseph Doherty did some good work with the figures for the *America* (figure 74) (the head was copied from the current United States silver dollar), and that for the *Imperial*, and the *Centennial*.[4] But none of them approach the pure classical excellence of the *Glory of the Seas*.

In Philadelphia Samuel Sailor carried on the tradition, but never attained the skill of Rush. His only known figure is the naval officer who has been shooting the sun over Rigg & Brother's nautical instrument store in Philadelphia since 1875.[5]

Chief of all the Down East shipbuilding centers was Bath where the Sewalls, William Rogers, Goss & Sawyer, the Pattens, and others annually turned out at least two or three large vessels each. While this was not duplicated in other cities, some Maine and Massachusetts shipbuilding towns, Thomaston, Searsport, Brunswick, Cutler, Chelsea, Boston, etc., came very close to it. Such production gave ample work for shipcarvers.

In Bath the best known carver was C. A. L. Sampson who possibly was trained by Nathaniel L. Winsor once of Duxbury, Massachusetts, and later of Bath. In 1847 Sampson was working in Boston; in 1865, in Bath. During the War between the States he served as a Lieutenant Colonel of the Third Maine Infantry. It was in the period after the War when Bath assumed the lead in shipbuilding that his best carving was executed. The head of the *Western Belle*, 1876, preserved at the Peabody Museum is a fine example of his work as is that of the *Belle of Bath*, 1877 (figure 75).

Among his other works were the *Belle of Oregon*, 1876, now at Webb Academy, and the head of the *Leading Wind*, Bath, 1874, in Portland, Oregon. Colonel Sampson died in 1881. He was succeeded by William Southworth (1826-1909) who had learned his trade in Portland. Later he worked in Brunswick, Damariscotta, and Newcastle before buying Sampson's business.[6] It was Southworth in partnership with Emery Jones who cut many of the heads of the Skolfield fleet, one of which, the head of the *Sam Skolfield 2nd* is to be seen at the Sailor's Haven, Charlestown, Massachusetts. Southworth is said to have executed over 500 heads during his career. Contemporary to him at Bath were two other carvers, Woodbury Potter (1845 - 1915) who had been trained under Sampson and one Newcomb. Neither of them did much figurehead work, specializing in the trailboards, billets, name boards and other small carved work for the countless schooners the Maine yards were annually launching.[7]

Emery Jones of Freeport, Southworth's one time partner, was a typical shipcarver. Born in Pownall in 1827, from boyhood he knew vessels almost as soon as he could walk around the shipyards watching the carpenters, the sparmakers, the caulkers and the painters. Like

Figure 74. Figurehead ship *America*.

Figure 73. Figurehead ship *Glory of the Seas*. Courtesy India House.

Figure 76. Design by Wm. Southworth for figurehead. Author's Collection.

Figure 75. Figurehead ship *Western Belle* by C. A. L. Sampson. Courtesy Peabody Museum of Salem.

most Maine coast boys he began working in the shipyard along with
his schooling and his farm chores. Marrying early in life and soon becoming a father, he applied himself to everything that offered an opportunity to better provide for his family. In addition to his shipcarving, he managed his farm, ran a livery stable, and carried the mail

Figure 77. Figurehead for ship *George R. Skolfield* in carver's shop. Courtesy Mrs.
Orra D. Jones.

twice a day from South Freeport to Freeport. "He was a very hard
working man", one of his descendants wrote, "always starting his day
between three and four o'clock in the morning and working until the
time he retired at night". Another who knew Mr. Jones said:

> I remember much about his shipcarving business as I lived near his shop.
> He was an excellent carver, doing work for shipbuilders in many places,
> Yarmouth, Bath, Brunswick, Damariscotta, etc. I used to hear him tell how
> he drove to Damariscotta, took the measurements of a ship and returned
> home to start the work, all the same day. I have seen him look at a picture
> or a pattern, then make a few quick strokes on the wood with a pencil,
> seize his chisel and mallet and soon the desired thing would take form. Mr.
> Jones was a fast worker and very deft in handling his tools. His work
> required huge amounts of glue and paint. He had a little paint mill and

always a pot of glue on the stove. Hundreds of dollars worth of gold beaten thin and placed between the leaves of a little book was used for gilding. Many times I have watched him slide the gold leaves with a brush onto the wood and smoothly brush them out. No sticking; no wrinkles. In those days there was no subterfuge about the work or materials, it had to be real. When one saw a gilded surface he knew it was coated with pure gold.[8]

The head of the *George R. Skolfield*, now in The Mariners' Museum is an example of Mr. Jones' work. Figure 77 shows it and the cutwater decorations in the carver's shop just after they had been completed in 1885. Mr. Jones died in 1908.

Another Maine carver who attained some degree of local fame was Edbury Hatch of Newcastle-Damariscotta. His training had come from William Southworth, who in 1870 certified ". . . that Edbury Hatch has served a regular apprenticeship of more than four years with me in the carving business, that he is honest, temperate and industrious . . . A lack of business is the only reason I do not employ him". So Hatch returned home to pick up what jobs he could until business improved. It did, but not enough to give all the carvers a living, and Hatch turned to farming and a job as night watchman in a hotel.[9]

His "pattern book", shown the author many years ago, indicates that although he carved a few full length figures, or at least was prepared with designs for them, most of his work must have been the billet heads, trailboards and stern ornaments for the increasing number of schooners in all sizes coming from the Maine shipyards.

On the Penobscot the best known were Thomas Seavey and his son and successor William L. Seavey of Bangor. The elder Seavey was in business by 1843 and in 1859 formed a partnership with his son. Thomas died or retired in 1886, but his son carried on until 1911. These two men must have executed a vast amount of carving for the many shipyards below Bangor, chiefly billet heads. Of these many examples are known to exist in the collections of the Peabody Museum and the Penobscot Museum.[10]

Portland, the principal city of Maine, was of course the home of many carvers. At least six had their own shops in operation from 1850 to the end of the century. Of them, the best known was Edward Souther Griffin, born 1834, died 1928. He learned his craft from his father, and about 1851 went into business for himself. With the exception of a short period while he followed the trade in Boston, he

Figure 78.   Design by Edbury Hatch.   Author's Collection.

Figure 79.   Billet head and trailboard by Edbury Hatch.   Author's Collection.

Figure 80. Billet head and stem decorations by Edbury Hatch. Author's Collection.

Figure 81. Stern designs by Edbury Hatch. Author's Collection.

Figure 82.   Stern designs by Edbury Hatch.   Author's Collection.

Figure 83.   Stern eagle design by Edbury Hatch.   Author's Collection.

worked in Portland until about 1900. In 1869 he was awarded a medal for a figurehead exhibited before the New England and Maine State Agriculture Society. One of his many apprentices was Joseph P. Mer-

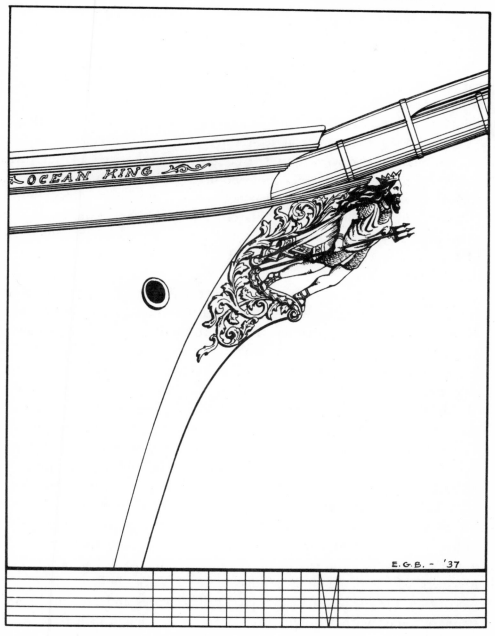

Figure 84. Figurehead ship *Ocean King*. From plan of vessel.

rill who later established his own shop in Portland.[11] Another Portland carver of no mean ability was Nahorn Littlefield who with his brother conducted an establishment from 1856 to 1878. One of his designs, that for the ship *Ocean King* (figure 84), built 1874, has been preserved.[12] The head of the ship *Rembrandt* in the Peabody Museum is thought to be from Littlefield's shop.

Maine produced many other carvers such as Henry Counce who carved for the vessels built at Thomaston; S. L. Treat who did the work for the Sawyer's of Millbridge; Richard Mace of Richmond, who cut the head for the *Theobold*; and James Todd of East Machias. Between 1850 and 1881 there were at least thirty-four shipcarvers working in the various Maine towns. But the period is characterized by but little grace and the Maine carvings show no originality of design. Mid-Victorian conventionalism had a firm hold on the craftsmen. The figures cut by Sampson, Southworth, Hatch, and Jones are remarkable for their similarity; the males all have the air of attending the obsequies of their best friends; the females, one of a hurried trip to the nearest obstetrician.

One of the grand men of the craft was John Bellamy, born at Kittery Point, Maine, in 1836. As a youth he studied art in Boston and New York and later apprenticed himself to the Boston shipcarver Laban S. Beecher. With his training completed he secured a berth at the Charlestown Navy Yard. While there his work attracted such favorable attention that a public exhibition of several of his carvings was held in Boston. Later he returned to his birthplace and began work at the Portsmouth Navy Yard. By that time the prevailing design for all naval work was the American eagle. Bellamy soon developed a remarkable ability in depicting the national symbol, and, in fact, made it his specialty to such an extent that his style is known today as the "Bellamy Eagle". Many examples have been preserved in all attitudes and for all purposes from figureheads and stern carvings to ornaments for public buildings, and churches. The best perhaps of the ship work is the head carved for the U.S.S. *Lancaster* (figure 85) now at The Mariners' Museum. This is a huge piece of work, built-up in many pieces to a wing spread of eleven feet. The wings and extremities are strongly joined with wrought iron straps. The design called for such a large head that Mr. Bellamy was forced to carve it in sections. Then

Figure 85. Figurehead U.S.S. *Lancaster* by John Bellamy. Courtesy Mariners' Museum.

when it was completed the several parts were assembled on the bow of the ship and bolted in place. One of Mr. Bellamy's relatives recalls vividly watching the whole process from the original "laying down" of the figure on the mould loft floor, through the carving of the individual pieces, and then the final assembly on the vessel. Another specimen was the *Niagara* head once at the Charlestown Navy Yard. Of course, with his constant work with the same motif, Bellamy developed marked characteristics, such as the deep concave wings, the square sectioned beak, and the heavily incised eye sockets. But notwithstanding this conventionalizing all his work shows great strength and individuality of pose. In 1902 he received the benefit of an annuity and retired from official work, continuing in his own shop until a year or two before his death (figure 86). He lived to be seventy-eight, dying in 1914, one of the most respected and beloved residents of Portsmouth.[13]

Figure 86.   John Bellamy's shop. Courtesy Joseph W. P. Frost.

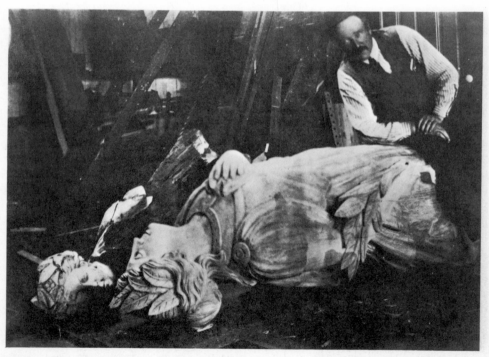

Figure 87.   Old and new figureheads ship *Falls of Clyde* by Edward Bell Lovejoy. Courtesy Mrs. Grace Lovejoy Faulkner.

On the Pacific Coast the shipbuilding business was not one which in the days of sail attained any considerable proportions. Shipcarving probably had its beginning in the winter of 1791-92 with the construction of the sloop *Adventure* at Vancouver Island by the crew of the ship *Columbia*. Describing her one of the officers wrote ". . . she is one of the prettiest vessels I ever saw, of about 45 tons, with a handsome figure head and false badges, and other ways touch'd off in high stile". Since this expedition carried a professional artist, George Davidson, it is quite possible the figurehead was designed by him. But whether he cut it, or left that to a more experienced tool handler, Samuel Yendell the shipcarpenter, is indeterminable.[14] From then until the middle part of the next century, shipbuilding was decidedly a minor industry, confined chiefly to small sloops and schooners, many of which were brought out from the Atlantic Coast in "knock-down" form. As late as 1880 San Francisco, the chief port, boasted of only one builder, Mathew Turner, whose establishment warranted much attention. But even after the sailing vessels had virtually disappeared from the Atlantic Coast, San Francisco continued to be the home port for dozens of hard worked Behring Sea whalers, salmon droghers, Island traders, and grain ships. Their long voyages around the Horn, across the Pacific, or into the Arctic ice brought a huge amount of repair work to the shipcarpenters, sparmakers, riggers, and shipcarvers.[15]

The first shipcarver definitely known to have practised the art in San Francisco after it became American territory was Louis A. Haehnlen. Nothing seems to have been preserved of his work. Following him came William Gereau who built up a business large enough to warrant the employment of two assistants, Thomas Carroll and Tarleton B. Earl. Contemporary to these men was a carver whose nationality makes him most intriguing, Mon Hon, a Chinese.[16]

But the best known shipcarver in San Francisco was Edward Bell Lovejoy. He was born there in 1857, and at the age of fifteen was apprenticed to his uncle, William Gereau. After Lovejoy had been given but two years of training Mr. Gereau died, leaving the business to the young man. The waterfront at San Francisco in the 'seventies was no place for a child. But despite that and despite the earthquakes and fires, until his death in 1917, Mr. Lovejoy was actively engaged in shipcarving, perhaps the last man following the art in America. Until Lovejoy came of age the

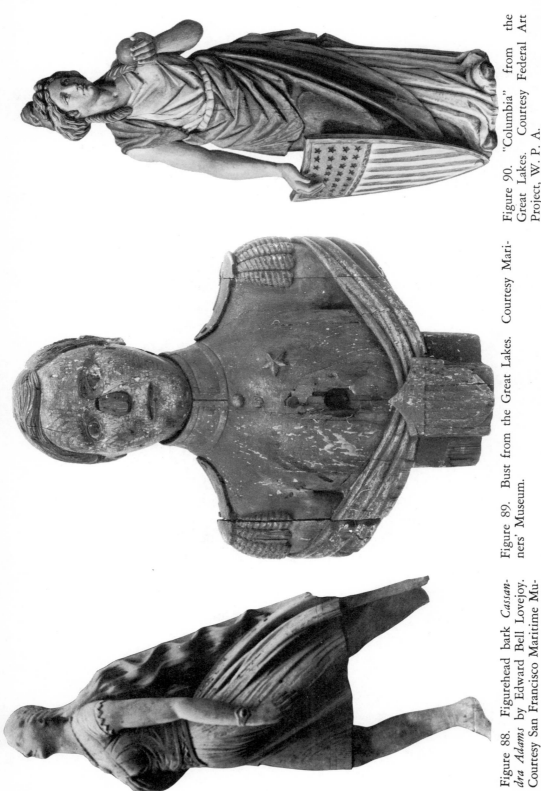

Figure 88. Figurehead bark *Cassandra Adams* by Edward Bell Lovejoy. Courtesy San Francisco Maritime Museum.

Figure 89. Bust from the Great Lakes. Courtesy Mariners' Museum.

Figure 90. "Columbia" from the Great Lakes. Courtesy Federal Art Project, W. P. A.

business was operated under the name of Gereau's widow, with Lovejoy acting as the man of business, supervising the work of the journeymen carvers, Paul Hubbard and Benjamin Luce. Although in his early years he did much original work for vessels built all along the Coast, his chief field in later days lay in the carving of figures for vessels whose heads had been carried away or damaged at sea. Figure 87 shows the fine type of work he executed, and illustrates his later business as well. In the background lies the shattered remains of the original figurehead of the ship *Falls of Clyde*. Just before it, with the carver himself seated on the base, is a new head, ready to be put on the bow of the vessel. Mr. Lovejoy cut this head, remarkable for the delicacy of the detail, from a huge block of hard maple which in the rough cost eight hundred dollars. Because so much of his work was replacement, it is particularly difficult to identify.[17]

Puget Sound in Washington was the scene of the largest Pacific shipyards devoted to new work. Many of the master builders, such as the Halls of Port Blakely, were originally from Maine and Massachusetts yards which had felt the depression following the War. These men accustomed to the skilled work of the Fowles, the Woodbury Gerrishs, or the Sampsons were forced to go to Mr. Lovejoy in San Francisco to find their equal. One of his heads, carved for a Puget Sound vessel, the bark *Cassandra Adams,* was built at Seabeck in 1876 and named for the owner's young daughter. This image is another which never went to sea for the short skirts and buxom figure did not fit Mr. Adams' somewhat Victorian ideas. Instead of placing it on the bow, he ordered another portrait cut "with less revealment and more modesty" (figure 88).[18]

On the Great Lakes, although most vessels were void of figureheads, there seems to have been some small amount of carving done. The first European vessel known to have been built on the Lakes was La Salle's *Griffin,* 1679. She is said to have carried some decorations but a figurehead is not specifically mentioned. From then on for 150 years nothing seems to be known about the art. After about 1740 a fairly large number of vessels were built, all of them seem to have been small sloops and schooners for which the iron work, rigging, and equipment were always imported from the Eastern seaboard towns. Carvings do not appear to have been entered on the orders, and if any were used, they must have been the work of amateur carvers among the shipcarpenters. Nor

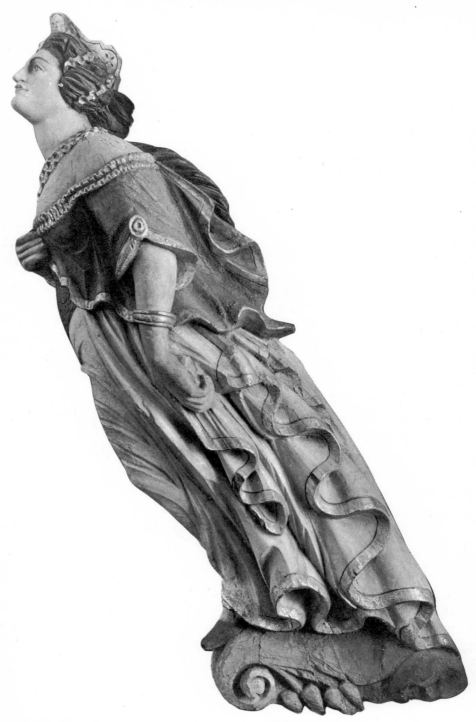

Figure 91. Figurehead ship *Edinburgh* by John Rogerson, 1883. Courtesy Addison Gallery.

are heads included in any of the descriptions of American men of war on the Lakes in the War of 1812. In fact, the first known head with Great Lakes associations is that of the steamer *Caroline,* ca. 1820, now preserved at the Buffalo Historical Society. That she was built on the Lakes is not definite, nor is it certain who did the carving. The workmanship is extremely good and has all the characteristics of those known to be from the hand of Jeremiah Dodge of New York City. If this is a correct attribution, it is not, of course, from the hand of a "fresh water" carver.[19]

The same lack of information is true of the few extant heads of vessels which sailed the Great Lakes. One, (figure 89) a bust now in The Mariners' Museum, was found floating in the Saint Clair River. It displays none of the skill found in the shops of some of the coastal carvers, and very probably represents the average output of the Great Lakes carvers. From the costume, a none too reliable criterion, it dates well after the period of the War between the States.[20]

At the other end of the quality scale of the Great Lakes carvings is a full length head now in a private collection (figure 90). This is a figure of "Columbia" in classical clothing with the shield of the United States at her side. Since the figure has undergone restoration, it is impossible to say with accuracy anything concerning the details of workmanship. It appears, however, to have been the product of a very skilled artisan who understood not only the technical limitations of his medium but also human anatomy and the basic principles of design. It is dated 1856 yet from the number of stars, thirty-six, on the shield the figure would date between 1867 and 1876. Again because of the restoration this is not reliable.

At least one well known seaboard carver, Laban S. Beecher of Boston, emigrated to the Lakes region. He is supposed to have executed considerable work before his death in 1876.[21]

While all the work and men mentioned heretofore, originated in the United States, one Canadian, John Rogerson, deserves some attention because he received his training here and also because he worked for vessels built in the States. Rogerson was born in Scotland in 1837. At the age of twelve he came to Boston to join his father who had previously emigrated. Finding his father dead, Rogerson moved to Saint John, New Brunswick, where his mother's brother, Edward Charters,

Figure 92. Billet head schooner *A. McNichol* by Holman Chaloner. Author's Collection.

Figure 94. "Indian", the best type of large vessel head. Courtesy Walter Muir Whitehill.

Figure 93. "Highlander" figurehead. Courtesy Peabody Museum of Salem.

lived. To him John Rogerson was apprenticed for a short time. After this preliminary training, he went to Boston, where he worked for two years with one of the leading shipcarvers, John D. Fowle. Then he returned to Saint John and entered business on his own account. At the height of his career the *London Shipping Journal* called him the "best workman on the other side of the Atlantic". This is probably an overstatement when one considers his existing work, all of which shows a most remarkable similarity in design and execution. In fact, the pieces have so little individuality that one is almost inclined to believe he used the same design time and time again, varying only the small details of dress ornaments. Examples of his work are to be found in the New Brunswick Museum, The Mariners' Museum, the Bourne Museum, the Kendall Whaling Museum, the Addison Gallery, Andover (figure 91), and in several private collections. Rogerson retired as a shipcarver in 1887, and, after working thirty years in the Saint John Custom House, died in 1925.[22]

Of all the men who followed the craft of shipcarver professionally not one is living today. The last was Holman Waldron Chaloner. As a boy in a Maine shipyard he learned how vessels were built and decorated during the hey-day of the "Down Easters" and he saw the time when shipbuilding and shipcarving came to their practical end. Chaloner's story pieced together from a series of letters is indeed the final chapter.

"I was born in 1851 in East Machias, Maine and from the age of 14 to 20 I worked summers in the ship yard and went to school winters. All the men knew me and I was the butt of all the jokes and fun especially as we would be sitting around eating dinner in the blacksmith shop.

"At first I worked with the painters around about and under the vessel's bottom with green or red or lead color for the first coat. Of all the painting one could do in a life time painting under the bottom of a vessel used to strike me as the worst. Looking and holding one's arm up for hours, the green liquid from the brush running down your arm into your neck, head and clothes. On the bottom of the brush we had to fasten a circle of leather 3 to 4 inches in diameter to catch the drippings, but some times when that would get full it would spill all over us. Because I tried to keep clean the other painters only made fun of me

Figure 95. "Victorian Girl" an average figurehead. Courtesy Peabody Museum of Salem.

and jokes. Mornings when we had to put on these paint clothes again for the day's work, after drying off all night it would be almost impossible to get them on.

"The other different painting around the vessel's I liked quite well and Mr. Lyman Hall, my boss, said I was doing nicely which was quite encouraging. When there was no painting I got to helping the carpenters; then the joiners; or with any thing that was to be done. One day Mr. Todd said me, "Hally you seem to be building the whole ship, would you like to help me a little on some rope moulding?" He showed me how to mark the lines and to cut the half round pine wood to look like 2½ inch rope. This was mostly on a circle to go around the stern and quarters. Then he showed me how to do the scrolls for stern ornament. Mr. James Todd was an Englishman and had learned from the several famous English carvers. I was finally worked into all the different carvings on a vessel. It was easy for me as I had always carved with knife or chisel and had made many carved things for our family and the children around us.

"As for the figure heads most of them by this time were for schooners. Some would be small and quite plain as to carving. Some of them were not cut in our yard since many of the Maine owners sent to Boston for their figure heads, and some owners in New York and other places would have them made at home and sent to the Maine yards. No sketches of figure heads were ever used the second time for no two were alike. Most were what we called Billet heads. Good ones would roll over and twist out at the top and sides with a skirt of scrolls, leaves or flowers up and down each side of the cutwater. The painter would gild the head, the flowers, the leaves, and scrolls on the raised carvings: all hollow places were painted red. I got up a head with the skirting to run down each side of the cut water. This was all my own idea and was done in my Father's shop near home. Mr. Lyman Hall the boss gilder who gilded it for us, was so pleased with it he said I aught to send it to the County Fair, and offered to take it there for me. Of all the carvings there mine took first prize. This head I sold to George Burral & Co. and they put it on their schooner *A. McNichol* in 1874 (figure 92).

"All my art is self taught, of my own way of thinking and without any thanks to any person except Mr. James Todd for teaching me

Dimensions of Figureheads and Lacing Pieces.

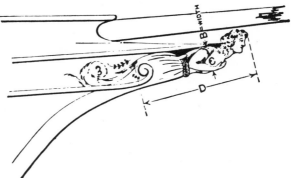

FIG. 12.

A LENGTH OF VESSEL, B. S.	B SIZE OF LACING PIECE.	C DEPTH OF FIGURE-HEAD.	D LENGTH OF FIGURE OUTSIDE OF STEM.	
Feet.	Inches.	Inches.	Feet.	Inches.
450	12¼	30¼	9	6
400	12	28½	9	0
350	11¼	26¾	8	6
300	10½	25	8	0
250	9¼	23¼	7	6
200	9	21½	7	0
150	8¼	19¾	6	6
100	7½	18	6	0

NOTE. — Angle of lacing piece, 45°.

Figure 96. The "standard" figure-head. From G. Simpson: *Naval Constructor.*

to carve in wood and for details connected with Carving. I do not think I aught to be classed as a carver of figure heads for I had not experience in that line although I could carve any order given me at that time. As ship work was slacking up for want of orders, I went to Boston to begin cabinet making. The very last work I did in East Machias was on a schooner named the *Susan & Phoebe*".[23]

As long as romantics go down to the sea under sail there will always be a few figureheads afloat. But these will not be sufficient in quantity ever to warrant even one man applying his entire time to the craft. The day of the figurehead and its creators is gone.[24]

Figure 97. Trail and quarter boards. Courtesy Maryland Historical Society.

VI
Miscellaneous Carvings

I N ADDITION to the head and stern decorations, numerous other
pieces of carved work might be found on almost any kind of vessel, sail and steam alike. Aside from the trailboards and name boards
very few of these miscellaneous carvings have been preserved and seldom were they shown in plans. It is therefore impossible to trace the
development of styles or to do much more than indicate what the pieces
were.

Trailboards, the pieces of carved work extending on each side
along the head knee from the figure or billet head to the hull, are mentioned in the Budd and Knight bill dated 1689 and continued in use
to the end of sailing vessel construction. Until the plans of the American
vessels purchased or captured by the British after the mid-eighteenth
century were found in the Admiralty we had no knowledge of the designs used on the Western side of the Atlantic. Fortunately in these
plans a few trailboards are depicted. These usually show conventional
designs of scrolls, foliage, crossed or draped flags, cannon, and national
shields. Occasionally human or animal figures were used and at times
the trailboard carvings were part of the figurehead itself. These same
designs prevailed as long as trailboards were used. Figures 12-15 show
the design of the trailboards used on the Revolutionary vessels and figures 50, 58, 79-80 demonstrate the continuity. Often the trailboards of
merchant vessels carried the name of the vessel as a part of the design.
This variety is seen in figure 97.

Another piece of head structure which frequently carried some
carved decorations were the naval "woods" or "hoods". These, popular from about 1820 to 1860, were planking which covered the space
from the upper (back) to the lower (foot) rails supporting the figurehead. The woods gave some weather protection and privacy when the
head was used as a necessary. The professional decoration on the ex-

c. U.S.C.G.S. *Bear*.

b. U.S.S. *Hartford*, ca. 1870.

a. U.S.S. *Michigan*, 1844.

Figure 98. Gang way boards. A. and c., courtesy Mariners' Museum; b, U.S. Naval Academy.

terior was usually simple, a few mouldings around the edges and perhaps the letters forming the name of the vessel, not even the traditional half-moons or vines. Figure 53 shows the naval woods on the *Seamans Bride*.

Names of the vessels inscribed in boards very frequently were fastened to the fore and after quarters along the rail. Forward they were at times called "head" boards and aft, "quarter" boards. They were usually simple to make them easily legible but fancy ends or scrolled decorations were to be found and some were highly carved. Laws stipulating that every documented vessel carry her name clearly lettered at least on the stern gave the carver another chance to show his skill with individual letters which were fastened to the transom or occasionally cut into planking. Because the applied letters were very fragile few have been preserved; those from the skipjack *Marie* in the Maryland Historical Society are one of the few complete sets in a public collection.

Breaks in the rails provided other opportunities for the carver. In the vessels of the eighteenth and early nineteenth centuries, carved blocks called "hance pieces" formed the transition between say the quarterdeck rail and the waist rail or the forecastle and the waist. On plans these blocks were usually shown as nothing more than a moulding terminating in a scroll. Being so simple the pieces have not attracted collectors. When gang ways through the high bulwarks of naval vessels and packet ships came into use the end faces of the bulwarks were finished off with "gang way boards". These were heavy pieces of some hard wood with a carved design generally symbolizing the name of the vessel. Many are to be seen in public collections but except for their dimensions, the earliest could have been used on the latest without the difference being noticed (figure 98).

Another hull decoration was to be found on the end of the cat head, the timber which projected from the forward quarters to serve as a crane boom when getting the anchors on the rail. From its earliest use, the outer end has been decorated in most instances with a lion's head in low relief. After about 1880 instead of a piece of carved wood, the decoration was an iron casting. Only one complete cat head of reasonably early vintage is known to exist. This, from the Salem owned ship *Saint Paul*, was salvaged during a rebuilding in 1849. It shows a conventionalized lion's head in full-round rather than an applied cat's

Figure 100. Wooden pattern for cast iron cat head face. Courtesy Old Sturbridge Village.

Figure 99. Wooden cat head face. Courtesy Hampton Galleries.

Figure 101. Cast iron cat head face U.S.S. *Brooklyn.*
Courtesy Peabody Museum of Salem.

Figure 102. Cast iron cat head face. Courtesy Kendall
Whaling Museum.

face on the end. Stars, panels, and other more or less conventional designs were also found on cat heads. Frequently in the eighteenth and nineteenth centuries cat heads were supported by carved knees or brackets. Possibly the two roughly triangular pieces of carved work in the Naval Academy Museum said to have been salvaged from the wreck of the frigate *Philadelphia* may be such brackets. None are positively known to exist (figures 43, 99-103).

Figure 103.   Cat head brackets Frigate *Philadelphia.*   Courtesy U.S. Naval Academy.

Overhanging ends on trunk cabins were also supported by similar carved knees. None have been found in public collections, but photographs of late nineteenth century examples are available. One is shown in figure 104.

Aloft everything was purely functional, until one reached the uppermost masthead. There the truck was to be found. In its simplest form it was nothing more than a disk of hard wood with one or two sheaves for signal or flag halliards. Other widely used trucks were ball, acorn, and onion shaped. In contrast with that simplicity, on Chesapeake Bay some mast heads were decorated lavishly. The foremast of the schooner *Mary J. Bond* carried a full length figure of that young lady. The schooner *Mattie F. Dean* had a similar figure, and the Brewington Collection in the Maryland Historical Society has a mast head figure of an 1890 angel complete with bustle. The name of the vessel from which it came is not known because the figure was found floating in the Bay after a storm and like Icarus had lost its wings in the fall. Another mast head decoration in the collection, this from the schooner *Eva,* is a cast metal piece representing King Edgar slaying the Saxons. Not in the collection but well remembered around the Bay were the capital "A" on the foremast head of the bugeye *Avalon* and the "L" on the fore and the joined "F P" on the main mast of the bugeye *L. F. Petty* (figures 105-108).

Below decks the cabin joiner work in general followed the prevailing architectural fashion of the period. Since plaster and wall paper were hardly suited to ship board use, the interior finish of the "home afloat" had to be translated into panels, pilasters, and cornices. In many of these the shipcarver had a share. That we know from descriptions of early cabins and photographs of late ones. For instance, in 1816: "The finish . . . maple and mahogany varnished; columns with gilt capitals . . . around . . . as a cornice is a row of gilt hatpins . . .". In 1851: ". . . The great cabin . . . Gothic panels of bird's eye maple, with frames of satin wood, relieved with zebra, mahogany and rose wood, enameled cornices edged with gold, and dark pilasters, with curiously carved and gilded capitals, and dark imitation marble pedestals . . .". Of the 1880's a shipcarver wrote: "Most of the cabins were paneled and had pilasters with hand carved capitals . . . The painters would gild them in gold leaf". Each of these gives some indication of the extent of interior carving, but few actual examples have been preserved. Those in figure 109 are from the collection in the Old State House, Boston. Several bills in the Fernald & Pettigrew papers show that at times stained glass windows were used. For instance, Hugh M. Falconer in 1847 supplied the ship *Columbus* with "stained & Enamelled Glass in bulkhead Sash, subject Landing of Columbus $20.00" and James West of New York two years later supplied the ship *Empire State* with "1 bulkhead Sash State Arms of N. Y. $25.00" and "16 Sash according to design selected at $4.00 each". While not carvings these indicate how elaborately the interiors of cabins were finished at the period.

One minor piece of interior carving was a motto fastened over the companionway ladder in some Chesapeake Bay craft. All of those seen were pious sentiments such as "In God We Trust", "God Bless

Figure 104. Cabin bracket.

Figure 105. Chesapeake Bay ship carvings. Top, quarter board; left and right, mast head figures; center, stern decorations; others, figureheads and billet heads. From Author's Collection, now Maryland Historical Society.

Figure 106. Trucks. From Author's Collection, now Maryland Historical Society.

Figure 107.   Mast head decoration, schooner *Mattie F. Dean.*

Figure 108.   Mast head decoration bugeye *Avalon.*

Figure 109.   Pilaster capitals.   Courtesy Bostonian Society.

Figure 110.   Mast sheath ship *New York*, 1822.   Courtesy Bourne Whaling Museum.

113

Our Home" or "God Save the Poor Sailor" surrounded by incised floral swags or sprays. These were not the work of professional carvers, but the scrimshawing of storm-bound amateurs.

When the rudder head or a mast passed through the open space of a cabin it was customary to enclose the more or less rough timber with a casing. Although this might be a simple box finished in panels matching the cabin bulkheads, it might be a highly carved casing such as that shown in figure 110, a unique piece now in the Whaling Museum, New Bedford. It came originally from the packet ship *New York* built in 1822 by Brown & Bell at New York.

On the deck itself the carver seldom had an opportunity to display his art. Out of sheer exuberance George Crowninshield had the full figure of an Indian chief, complete with quiver of arrows standing on the deck of his yacht *Cleopatra's Barge*. When the *Barge* was cruising in Mediterranean waters, like the images carried by many vessels owned in Roman Catholic countries, it was the object of veneration by visitors who believed it to be the representation of an American saint. Of real use was the life-sized carved figure of a sailor dressed in "wide pants and flap collar" holding a steering compass in his hands which served as the binnacle of the clipper *Champion of the Seas*. It went down with the ship when she was lost off Cape Horn in 1876. Another similar binnacle was once in the possession of a well-known firm of instrument makers.

After the North River Steamboat of Claremont proved the practicality of its type of propulsion, steamers developed with great rapidity. Within a decade they were in use on rivers and bays wherever the volume of traffic warranted and the conquest of the Atlantic was beginning. At first the majority with the addition of the engine, boilers and paddle wheels, were nothing more than an adaption of the sailing vessel, even to the decorations. When the raked stem of the sailing vessel gave way to the plumb stem and all the complications of the head with its knees, rails and trailboards disappeared, vestigal figureheads were retained for a while. Even as late as the 1850's the Collins Liners had tiny figures on their stem heads, but as these were incongruous and insignificant the use of such figures was quickly dropped on merchant vessels. On naval vessels with metal hulls the traditional figurehead was retained, though seldom, if ever, were the figures the work

Figure 111. Steamboat paddle box decoration, Boston harbor ferry. Courtesy Massachusetts Institute of Technology.

Figure 112. Steamboat paddle box decoration. Courtesy Peabody Museum of Salem.

Figure 113. Pilot house eagle.

of shipcarvers, but rather that of sculptors, for instance the head of the U.S.S. *Massachusetts,* was the work of Saint Gaudens. All the decorations were of cast iron or bronze. In 1909 the Secretary of the Navy ordered these removed. Since then no carved work of any type has been used.

Since the paddle wheels threw much water on the deck and were constant dangers to anything in their vicinity, they were soon covered by "boxes". The faces of these large semi-cylindrical enclosures offered a fine space for decoration. In the early years the name of the vessel was the sole addition. Next when it was discovered some means of equalizing pressure on unevenly immersed paddle wheels was necessary, "breathers" were added. These were nothing more than louvered openings which took a variety of shapes: squares, ovals, triangles, diamonds, and others, with any form of moulded frame the builder might choose. And from these fancy breathers developed the sunbursts, domes, vistas, and whatnots of the later days. The most commonly found decorations were the sunbursts, radial designs emanating from a central lunette usually carved in relief. Because of the size of the complete decoration — between thirty and forty feet diameter — none

Figure 114. Pilot house and stack decorations. Courtesy Peabody Museum of Salem.

have been preserved in their entirety but many of the lunettes have been (figures 111-112).

Another radical departure from the sailing vessel was the shift of the master and the steering wheel from the quarter deck at the extreme stern to the forward end of the steam vessel. Houses were soon built over the steering wheels to give the helmsman and master some weather protection, and perhaps to emphasize the importance of the wheel-house, decorations were added to the tops. At first these figures were carved full round; later they became little more than silhouettes; still later the spread eagle completely dominated until the electric search-light seized its place and ended all decoration. In the last days the eagles, like as not, were metal castings rather than wood carvings (figure 113).

Of course just as there were eccentrics ashore such as "Lord" Tim-othy Dexter who embellished domestic architecture with all manner of ridiculous carvings, there were some afloat. An example is shown in figure 114. No traditional, functional, or decorative value can be

Figure 115. Billet heads, left pair about 1830; right pair about 1860. Courtesy Peabody Museum of Salem.

Figure 116. Billet heads, left pair about 1880; right pair about 1900. Courtesy Peabody Museum of Salem.

found for the strange apparition suspended between sky and vessel. At the best one can only say it provided some craftsman with a job for a few days or hours.

The Figureheads
of the Frigate *Constitution*

I F ALL the ink expended in writing about the most famous of United States men of war, the frigate *Constitution*, were poured into one place, there would doubtless be enough to float the ship. In that sea, the portion devoted to her figureheads would make more than a wave but have as little substance as its froth and foam. Because the frigate has played so great a role in our naval tradition and because she has had so many figureheads, an accurate history of them and their carvers is worth telling.

In 1794 the Congress of the United States decided to build a Navy, or at least six frigates.[1] At that time there was no naval establishment; consequently the work of building the vessels was handed to private shipyards spread along the coast from Norfolk, Virginia to Portsmouth, New Hampshire.[2] Not until 1795 was any thought given to naming the vessels. On February 20 of that year Joshua Humphreys wrote to the Secretary of War submitting ideas on proper names. After due consideration the name *Constitution* was selected for the frigate building at Boston.[3] With the name chosen William Rush of Philadelphia was asked to present ideas for the figurehead designs of each. These he sent to Humphreys, the Chief Naval Constructor, on April 30, 1795. Humphreys forwarded them to the Secretary of War for approval. The portion referring to the figure for the *Constitution* was:

> As the *Constitution* of the Empire is the result of the Union of the States and united begetts Strength it aught to be represented by an Herculean figure standing on the firm rock of Independence resting one hand on the fasces, which was bound by the Genius of America and the other hand presenting a scroll of paper, supposed to be the Constitution of America with proper appendages, the foundation of Legislation.[4]

On September 20, 1796 the Secretary of War wrote the Secretary of the Treasury: "Mr John Skillen of Boston has been mentioned to me

Figure 117. Attack on Tripoli by Corne, 1804. Courtesy U.S. Naval Academy.

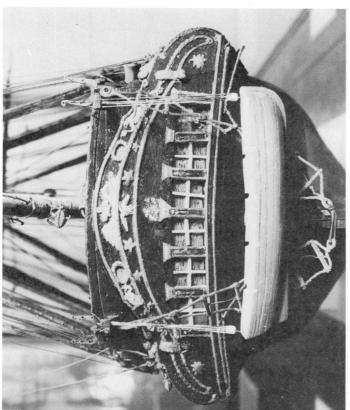

Figure 119. Stern of Commodore Hull's model U.S.S. *Constitution*, 1813. Courtesy Peabody Museum of Salem.

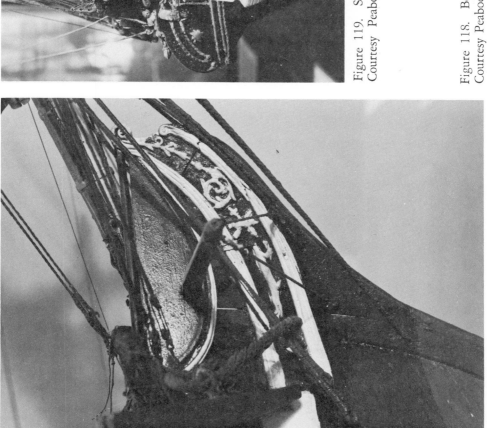

Figure 118. Bow of Commodore Hull's model U.S.S. *Constitution*, 1813. Courtesy Peabody Museum of Salem.

by Mr Rush, as a qualified artist to undertake the carving of the head of figure for the Frigate building at that Town . . . There is a drawing of the figure (a Hercules) now preparing which I shall forward to Mr Skillen, as soon as finished".[5]

Unfortunately neither that drawing nor any contemporary picture or model of the frigate has been preserved to show us what the figure was like. But we do know beyond a shadow of doubt that Skillin did the work because the bill of "John & S[imeon] Skill[in] for carving $719.33" was paid and earmarked *Constitution*.[6] Further we know the basic design was followed because on May 31, 1797 the Reverend Dr. Bentley of Salem wrote in his diary:

> saw the new Ship . . . the Head called Constitution. finished by Skillings. It is an Hercules with the fasces of the United States & the Constitution standing upon a rock & his battoon lying beneath him.[7]

As for the stern decorations, there is not a word of description by Rush, Bentley, or the journalists. Originally it had been suggested that all six frigates "should be all alike to shew they belong to one family and represented by an Eagle in the Center with the Constellations around him, supported on each Quarter by the Figures of Liberty and Justice".[8] This plan was not followed *in toto*, although the three principal elements were included in those sterns we know. The best and most reliable representation of the stern in its first state is in the view of the Attack on Tripoli in 1803 painted by Corne who certainly saw the *Constitution*. It shows heavy quarter-piece figures and less clearly other ornaments (figure 117).[9]

So dressed the frigate was launched, fought through the war with France and through most of the war with the Barbary Pirates. It has been written time after time that Hercules was shot away in one of the attacks on Tripoli and replaced by a figure of Neptune.[10] But the frigate's log records otherwise. On September 12, 1804 she was in collision with the United States frigate *President*. The survey showed among other damage "our figure head broken to pieces".[11] Commodore Preble sent the frigate to Malta at once for repairs and the log entry on September 25 tells us, "nine carpenters came on board . . . employed this forenoon in taking down the Figurehead which is cut to pieces & thrown away as useless".

What replaced it? A Neptune? Not at all, for the First Lieutenant of the frigate, Charles Gordon, wrote Commodore Preble from Malta on September 29 that "The Cut Water and Billet Head will be finished in 6 or 7 days".[12] The log states on October 10, " . . . carpenters . . . fitting the Billet Head"; on October 18, "This forenoon the Cut Water & Billet head were completed".[13] Unless one is prepared to prove the First Lieutenant of the frigate could not distinguish a billet from a figure, the constant use of "billet" in both log and letter should dispose

Figure 120.   Quarter Gallery Hull model. Courtesy Peabody Museum of Salem.

of the Neptune tradition. And finally on October 19 the log reads "The *Constitution* had before a Hercules head", thus Rush's design is further confirmed and the continuity established.[14] The name of the carver is not given. Doubtless he was a Maltese or English dockyard workman.[15]

Back to the United States went the frigate after her Mediterranean duty, and no changes have been traced until the great naval repair program began in 1807. The *Constitution* came in for her share and on July 18, 1808 the following bill was submitted to the Naval Agent at New York:

> To Daniel N. Train Dr.
>
> To Carving a Billet Head, with figures - quarter pieces with Bust etc upper and lower finishings for Gallery, one pair trusses for Stern pr [pair] Bracketts for Quarters, six pieces Quarters, six pieces of Garnishings for front of Gallery and two Stars for Stern for U. S. Ship Constitution $650.00
>
> Approved.[16]

But even these pieces were not the whole of the carved decorations for on June 16, 1808 Messrs Skillin [Simeon III] & Dodge of New York had already submitted a bill "U. S. Constitution To Carving two trail boards $40.". To this charge the Navy Agent also gave his approval.[17]

Obviously the entire decoration of the galleries and the stern were changed but no picture of the frigate which can be matched to the items in the bill has been found. The closest approach is Commodore Hull's model of 1813 in the Peabody Museum (figures 118-120).

With those carvings the frigate entered the War of 1812, the period of her greatest glory. Yet although her victories over H.M.S. *Guerrière*, *Cyane* and *Levant*, and *Java* were commemorated in prints and paintings not only in the United States but also in France, Denmark and England, not one of the pictures gives a clear representation of the "Billet Head, with figures" carved by Daniel N. Train. Some of the pictures do show a billet head sufficiently different from the conventional billet to warrant attention. These pictures are the ones by Michele Felice Corne working in Salem and Boston, Thomas Birch in Philadelphia, and E. W. Hoger at Elsinore. Each of these men was basing his work on contemporary knowledge of the vessel. On the other hand, Antoine Roux of Marseilles, and Montardier of Le Havre, show in their pictures of these actions a figurehead, a carving they could have known

Figure 122. Billet head in Peabody Museum. Courtesy Peabody Museum of Salem.

Figure 121. Billet head attributed to U.S.S. *Constitution* and to U.S.S. *Cyane* (I). Courtesy U.S. Navy Department. Note similarity of dragon to that in trailboard of Hull model.

Figure 123. Beecher's figure and Dodge's cranium
of Andrew Jackson, 1834. Courtesy Museum of the
City of New York.

only the when the frigate was in French waters during the Barbary Wars before 1804. And of course the paintings of the British artists could at the best have been based only on descriptions with the billet head a detail too unimportant in the whole composition to come in for mention other than by a single word. What Train's billet may have been can only be conjectured, based on the pictures by Birch, Corne and Hoger. The figure may been a bust of Preble, the naval hero of the pre-1812 period, or it may have been a figure symbolizing the constitution, the foundation of American law and government. Each of the three artists, working independently at widely separated points produced pictures of a carving obviously the same in design.

During the three actions with the British frigates the *Constitution* was hit by solid shot time after time and her commanding officers, Hull, Bainbridge and Stewart, submitted damage reports to the Navy Department. Not one of these has been found; therefore we do not know positively if Train's billet head was replaced. But it must have been, probably after the engagement with H.M.S. *Guerrière* because in no other way can one account for the plain scroll on Commodore Hull's own model and the identical billet in the Lynn-Bowen engraving. It should, however, be noted that in the Hull model the trailboards include figures which closely resemble the dragon in the billet head long claimed to have been on the *Constitution* at some time (figure 121). Perhaps this was Train's "Billet head with figures" and was replaced for some reason now unknown by the plain scroll billet so closely like the billet attributed to the *Constitution* at the Peabody Museum,[18] one possibly removed in 1834 (figure 122). There was damage to the stern as Surgeon Amos A. Evans wrote in his journal after the action "*Guerrière* . . . came against our stern with her bows twice and . . . injured our Taffrail", how extensive the damage was and whether it was replaced is not known.[19]

The first indication of a new head that can be found until the early 1830's is when the Navy proposed to scrap the frigate and Oliver Wendell Holmes with his famous poem "Ay, tear her tattered ensign down" so aroused the country, the vessel was saved and rebuilt. This time the head was altered. The new one sparked a controversy of surprising proportions and results.

Commodore Jesse D. Elliott was placed in command of the Boston Navy Yard in 1833 with orders to rebuild the frigate as she "originally

Figure 124. U.S.S. *Constitution* with Beecher head. Courtesy U.S. Navy Department.

was." On arrival he found "her bow decorated with a billet head" and "proceeded to have a figure made of that classic hero", Hercules.[20] While the work was underway, President Andrew Jackson visited the city and received such an enthusiastic reception from the citizens that Elliott sought permission from the Secretary of the Navy to substitute a figure of Old Hickory for Hercules. The Secretary gave it and the carving proceeded. The work was executed by Laban S. Beecher, a full figure of the President in heroic size, standing bare-headed with tall hat in hand, and a cloak draped close to the body, a costume said to be Jackson's riding habit.[21] On March 20, 1834 Beecher informed Elliott that he had been offered $1,500.00 to allow the figure to be stolen and that it was not safe in the carver's shop. It was therefore moved to the Navy Yard and Beecher completed the carving behind the walls. His charge was $300.00, just one fifth of the bribe offered.[22] On April 28, 1834 Jackson was placed on the *Constitution* (figure 123). At the same time Beecher commenced the head a new set of stern carvings was ordered for the frigate. No bill for this work has been found, but Elliott reported it included busts of Hull, Bainbridge and Stewart. These carvings were never placed on the stern.[23] Its appearance is shown in a good water color by W. A. K. Martin dated 1837 (figure 128).

As soon as the figure of Jackson was placed on the vessel there were threats to mutilate it, even to cause more serious damage. These induced Elliott to move the frigate to a mooring between two ships of the line then lying off the Yard. In spite of armed sentries on all three vessels during the night of July 2 in the midst of a violent thunder storm a young man named Samuel W. Dewey of Falmouth, Massachusetts, somehow rowed unseen out to the frigate and after two attempts sawed off the cranium at a point just below the nose (figure 127).[24] The next day the uproar was both loud and furious as pro- and anti-Jacksonians fumed or laughed. Journalists, caricaturists (figures 124-126) and ballad writers took up the battle. The Secretary of the Navy visited the Boston Yard and ordered the mutilated figure covered with canvas as long as the frigate remained in the Yard. On March 3, Commodore Elliott took command of the frigate and with a five stripe United States flag draped over the decapitated figure sailed for New York.[25] There, Elliott following his propensity for causing trouble, stepped on the toes of Commodore

The Decapitation of a great Blockhead by the Mysterious agency of the Claret coloured Coal.

Figure 125. Cartoon representing the decapitation of the Beecher head. Courtesy Peabody Museum of Salem.

THE NATIONAL BARBER.

Nat...pass along the knowledge box...that son of a gun snores so loud, he will wake the Commodore.

Figure 126. Cartoon of Dewey cutting off the Beecher cranium. Courtesy Bostonian Society.

Figure 127. The Beecher cranium, present whereabouts unknown. Photo Peabody Museum of Salem.

Ridgely, commandant at New York, who at once (March 9) dispatched a letter to the Navy Commissioners:

> The Constitution arrived this morning, as I am informed by Commodore Elliott, inside the Hook . . . I am directed by the Secretary of the Navy to have her figurehead repaired or completed, and had taken some steps to its completion but I am informed by Mr. Dodge, the Carver, that he had commenced on the block (preparatory) by an order from Com. Elliott from Boston. As it is not only usual, but actually premptory, by the regulations for the service, as well as by the law constituting your Board, that all instructions relating to the alteration, improvement &c of the Navy should emanate from the Navy Commissioners, Will you instruct me? Mr Dodge says if he merely replaces that part of the head decapitated, it will probably not detain her longer than a fortnight, but to do justice & give a whole figure, six weeks will not be too short . . .[26]

This letter, acknowledged by Mr. Secretary Dickerson on March 13, went on to instruct Commodore Ridgely ". . . no more is wanted than that so much of the Figurehead as has been removed should be restored which certainly can be done in two days . . .".[27] Then the final word on the headless horseman came in the New York *Daily Advertiser* of March 16:

> On Saturday forenoon [March 14] the head carved by Messrs Dodge & Sons of this city, was placed on the trunk representing president Jackson, on the bow of the frigate Constitution.[28]

That same day the frigate sailed for France, but not before Elliott had

Figure 128. Stern of the U.S.S. *Constitution* drawn by W. A. K. Martin in 1837. Courtesy Peabody Museum of Salem.

Figure 129. Fowle's figure of Andrew Jackson, 1846. Courtesy U.S. Naval Academy.

Figure 130. Billet head by Dialogue used in the 1876 restoration.

Figure 131. Billet head used in the 1906 restoration.

Figure 132. Present billet head.

written the Secretary, "The Artist employed to restore the figurehead has performed that service in a style reflecting credit on his patriotism and taste; and I pronounce the likeness even truer to the original than the one put on the figure in Boston".[29]

One would have thought the Navy had had its fill of Jackson figureheads, and indeed some of its officers had. Commodore Shubrick writing from Gosport (Norfolk) January 20, 1842 to the Commissioners complained that Old Hickory was in the way of the ship's work and that he wanted to remove him, substituting a billet head. The Commissioners replied instantly not to do it, change the angle of inclination yes, but no cutting or removing.[30]

In December 1846 the frigate then in the Boston Yard was again in need of repairs and before the work had been completed two years later, Jackson with body by Beecher and head by Dodge had been removed by the Boston carvers, J. D. and W. H. Fowle. Another figure of Jackson, a far better one, (figure 129) was carved by them, the bill being:[31]

For Carving Figure Head	$250.00
" fitting moulds for do	2.00
" carving trail boards	75.00
" 12 lbs. Copper bolts for F. Head	3.00
	$330.00

This figure carried her through the Civil War, in fact lasted longer than any other, down to the rebuilding of 1874 in Philadelphia. Then the Jackson by Fowle was removed, set up as a Navy Yard decoration, and finally sent to the Naval Academy where it remains.[32]

In its place the constructor hoped to put the 1812 billet head which was said on November 4, 1875 to be in the Navy Yard at Boston. On November 8 it was ordered to the frigate, but on May 31, 1876 the billet was found to be rotten and the constructor tried to get the Jackson head back. That failed and on June 23, 1876 John Dialogue, a Camden, New Jersey shipbuilder, offered with no allusions to 1797, 1804, 1812, or any other period to furnish a new billet head at a cost not to exceed $200.00.[33] That Dialogue did. In 1906 another restoration was undertaken by Rear Admiral Elliot Snow, C.C., U.S.N. who reported that the billet head he used was a copy of that carried in 1812, but how he knew exactly what that was is not disclosed.[34] He used a copy of the forked-tongued-dragon-which-faces-aft billet. And in the last, the 1926, restoration under Lieutenant John A. Lord, C.C., U.S.N. the piece is a "fiddle head . . . very similar to that removed from the ship in 1906 [Dialogue's 1876 job] with slight alteration in its contour" (figures 130-134).[35]

So far as one can determine from the many photographs taken from 1858 on to the present there was little or no change in the trailboards after the 1834 rebuilding, a conventionalized scroll design. No trace of the early boards has been found: the original set was removed at Malta in 1804 when Hercules was replaced; those of the 1906 restoration are owned by the Peabody Museum. In each successive rebuilding the stern decorations have been simplified and juggled around, but the stars, eagle, and pilasters of Martin's water color of 1837 are still to be seen.

Figure 133.   Present cat head face.

Figure 134.   Present gang way board.

There are many billets said to have been used on the *Constitution*. One is fixed on the bow and two are exhibited aboard the frigate; another is in the Peabody Museum; and the 1925 Catalog of the United States Naval Academy lists three more. Of the three on the frigate that on the bow was carved for the present restoration, 1926; one came from the 1876 rebuilding and was furnished by Dialogue; the last is from the 1906 restoration. The Director of the Naval Academy Museum states that the 1925 Catalog is in error; two of the billets are actually bronze label plates from billets and that the one billet at Annapolis is from H.M.S. *Cyane*. This identification apparently is based on Lossing's *Field Book of* 1812 and on Drake's *Old Landmarks of Boston*. It should, however, be noted that the trailboards of the Hull model made in 1813 include the same dragon motif found in the so-called *Cyane* billet, captured in 1815. And further, such a billet would correspond with the Train "billet with figures", and could have been removed from the *Constitution* when repaired after the action with H.M.S. *Guerrière*. The Peabody billet, the gift of the Eastern Yacht Club, could then have come from the late 1812 period, removed by Elliott in 1834. The records of the Navy Department, the Boston Navy Yard and the Eastern Yacht Club fail to prove anything conclusively.

Notes and References

CHAPTER I.

[1]*Virginia Company,* I, 523.

[2]Dow and Robinson, *Sailing Ships of New England,* I, 11.

[3]Hall, *Report,* 59.

[4]Ibid. 49; Maryland *Archives* XXV, 585 ff.

[5]Sutherland, *The Ship builder's Assistant,* 62. "The head of a Ship serves for little else than Ornament (for several Ships have no Heads) since its chiefest Conveniency is to tack the Weather Clew of the Foresail forward, to gammon the Bowsprit, to water the Provision, and for Houses of Ease . . . ". "Head" as used here means the entire structure forward of the stem, not the figure alone. Sutherland continues by designing a head. (See figure 3). "Fig. B represents the Head of a Ship of 1000 Tuns, the upper Rail a. being curved by the Method of a Sheel or Circle. However the Center 2. sweeps the middle Part, and 3.4. the other two Parts, only forward the Curve is reversed, and 5. sweeps that which makes the Top of the Crown, tho' sometime the upper Rail is ended as the Arch 15. described. 10. sweeps the Poll of the Lyon. 10. & 11. the aft Part of the Locks, 4. the Breast, 12. the Back. The other Parts of the Lyon are formed straight before it's carved. And after such a Fashion may every part of a Lyon be rough shaped. 6. sweeps the middle Rail b. 7. the Lower Rail c. and 9. the Raking. or Lower Part of the Supporter, answering the lower Rail. 8. sweeps the upper part of the Lace, to which the upper Cheek is fastened. 1. sweeps the cutting down of the Knee, and 13. the foremost part of the Knee. After such an intelligible manner may every part of any Head be demonstrated, without so many confused and perplexed Methods as are customary".

[6]Dow and Robinson, *Sailing Ships of New England,* I, 31; Hall, *Report,* 60.

[7]*Suffolk Deeds,* Liber VIII, 33.

[8]*Ibid.* V. 533; XII, 234.

[9]South Carolina *Gazette,* April 9, 1750.

[10]Maryland *Gazette,* January 31, 1760.

[11]South Carolina *Gazette,* September 6, 1773.

[12]Carr-Laughton, *Old Ships Sterns and Figureheads,* 63 ff.

[13]Massachusetts *Archives,* XXXV, 377; John Norris Letter Book, II, 178.

[14]John Norris Journal, 1709-11.

[15]Salem Custom House Records, Peabody Museum, pp 384, 465, 471.

[16]Perley, *History of Salem,* II, 386; III, 86, 397.

[17]John Reynell Journal.

[18]John Reynell Receipt Book; Logan Papers, 18, 106. Wilkinson also was given the job of decorating the magnificent barge Thomas Penn used to commute between Philadelphia and his country estate up the Delaware River: "Mr. Tho. Pen Dr. Augt 1733 to Cuting ye freese for his Barge & the Cote of Armes £6. 15. 0.". Bill in Penn Manuscripts, Accounts, I, 23.

[19]John Reynell Correspondence.

[20]John Reynell Receipt Book.

[21]Portsmouth, New Hampshire, Atheneum; Pepperell Papers, Portsmouth Historical Society.

[22] Maryland *Gazette*, August 30, 1745.
[23] *Boston Records Commission*, XXIX.
[24] *Daughters of the American Revolution Magazine*, November 1927, 745.
[25] Currier, *Ould Newbury*, 493.
[26] Dow and Robinson, *Sailing Ships of New England*, I, 30.
[27] Wharton-Storey Papers.
[28] *Shuldham Despatches*, 116.
[29] Watson, *Annals*, I, 575.
[30] Charles Wharton Day Book, June 1, 1776.
[31] Shaw Papers, Yale University.
[32] Illustrated in Brewington, *Chesapeake Bay*, 119.
[33] Admiralty Plan.
[34] Admiralty Plan.
[35] Admiralty Plans.

CHAPTER II.

[1] Carr-Laughton, *Old Ships Sterns and Figureheads*, 83.
[2] Connarroe Collection, Hancock to Cushing.
[3] *Journals Continental Congress*, December 13, 1775.
[4] Admiralty Draught, *Raleigh*, National Maritime Museum.
[5] *Essex Institute Historical Collections*, LXXIII, 258; *Antiques*. Oct. 1956, 362.
[6] Historical Society Ould Newbury Mss. Collections.
[7] Admiralty Draught, *Iris*, late *Hancock*; Admirals Despatch, 487, August 28, 1777.
[8] Admirals Despatch, 487, August 28, 1777. So many of the figureheads which have been preserved are today painted a glaring dead white that the casual observer is led to believe all heads were painted to resemble a piece of Cararra marble statuary. That impression is far from accurate. With the carving finished the craftsman called in a painter who under the direction of the master, colored the figure. A few heads were undoubtedly white, but the great majority were as one carver described them "painted to the life"; that is, in natural colors. The lions of the English and American vessels were yellow. White seems to have been the favorite color for the horse figureheads, possibly out of deference to the steeds which drew Neptune's chariot. It was also used when the ship was being repainted by the crew or by unskilled workmen. Most of the white heads, whenever the outer coat is removed, disclose an image "painted to the life".
[9] Admirals Despatch, 487, August 28, 1777.
[10] Admiralty Draught, *Cormirant*, (late the *Rattlesnake*).
[11] Ibid., *Confederate* late *Confederacy;* Shaw Papers, Yale University; Wolcott Papers, Massachusetts Historical Society.
[12] Boston Records Commission X, 247; Pennsylvania State Library R.P. Va. 60; Pennsylvania *Archives* 2nd., I, 155; 2nd., II, 266; Joseph Carson Receipt Book, April ?5, 1777.
[13] New York City *Directories; Minutes Common Council*, New York.
[14] Shaw Papers, Yale University; Wolcott Papers, Massachusetts Historical Society; Caleb Davis Papers, Connecticut Historical Society.
[15] Hudson Papers, New York Public Library.
[16] Bentley *Diary*, II, 328.
[17] Joshua Humphreys Correspondence.
[18] Bentley *Diary*, II, 328.
[19] Ibid., II, 452; Jones, *Ships of Kingston*, 43; Porter, *Rambles in Old Boston*, 206.
[20] Mss. Notes for a Life of John Peck, by D. Foster Taylor; Caleb Davis Papers.
[21] Connecticut State Library, Ship *Defense* Accounts.

[22]*New Haven Genealogical Magazine,* 999.

[23]Pennsylvania *Archives,* 2nd., I, 155.

[24]*New England Historical Genealogical Register,* XXXI, 393.

[25]Navy Board Eastern District Letter Book.

[26]Sutherland, *The Ship builder's Assistant,* 62.

[27]Independence Hall, Philadelphia; Joshua Humphreys Note Book.

[28]Peabody Museum, *Catalog Marine Room,* 125.

[29]*Essex Institute Historical Collections* (McIntire Number), XCIII, 122 ff.

[30]Bentley, *Diary,* II, 452.

[31]McIntire Papers.

[32]Derby Papers.

[33]McIntire Papers.

[34]*Essex Institute Historical Collections,* op. cit., quoting *Essex Gazette* April 20, 1811.

[35]Admiralty Plans, National Maritime Museum; National Archives Plans, *Randolph* and 74-gun ship.

CHAPTER III.

[1]*Pennsylvania Magazine of History,* XXXI, 381-82.

[2]Watson, *Annals,* I, 575.

[3]Dunlap, *History of Design,* I, 374-75.

[4]Pennsylvania *Archives,* 1st. XVIII, 675.

[5]Philadelphia *Directory,* 1785.

[6]Chandler, *Ship Building in Pennsylvania,* 29.

[7]Joshua Humphreys Accounts, 1773-95; Watson, *Annals,* I, 575.

[8]Hazard, *Register,* II, 374.

[9]Scharf & Westcott, *History of Philadelphia,* III, 2337.

[10]Watson, *Annals,* I, 575.

[11]Philadelphia Custom House Papers, 1784-85.

[12]Ricketson, *New Bedford,* 60.

[13]Watson *Annals,* I, 575.

[14]Navy Department Library, "Area File".

[15]Joshua Humphreys Correspondence.

[16]*American Daily Advertiser,* March 4, 1794.

[17]Sail plan of the frigate *Philadelphia,* Lenthall Papers, Franklin Institute. No single block of wood could be obtained sufficiently large to enable cutting such heads in their entirety. Therefore the block was built up from many smaller pieces, all carefully joined with trunnels. Parts which extended beyond the figure in the clear, such as arms, ornaments, etc., were carved separately and fitted to the figure with dovetail slip joints. These pieces were customarily unshipped when a vessel went to sea and were replaced only when she entered the quiet waters of a port. An excellent example of this is found in the figurehead of the U.S.S. *Hornet,* the design of which has been preserved in the Navy Department Archives. For harbor use an eagle holding a shield was in place, at sea a billet head was substituted.

[18]Stephen Girard Receipt Book; Rush bills in Girard Papers.

[19]Philadelphia *Daily Advertiser,* June 8, 1799.

[20]Ibid., May 25, 1799.

[21]Ibid., December 4, 1799; Mason, *Newport,* 134.

[22]*Quasi-War,* II, 408.

[23]Philadelphia *Daily Advertiser,* June 5, 1799.

[24]*Quasi-War,* III, 314.

[25]*Federal Gazette,* August 9, 1799; Joshua Humphreys Correspondence; Navy Department Library, Mss.

[26]*Quasi-War,* I, 356.

[27]Marceau, *Works of William Rush,* 20, 81.

[28]Boston *Directories;* Boston *Almanacs.*

[29]Old State House, Boston; Museum of the City of New York; Peabody Museum.

[30]Boston *Directories; Antiques,* December 1931; Ward Papers. Placing the figure on the vessel and seeing that it was securely fastened was usually a part of the work of the carver. And properly so since had it been left to the shipcarpenters, it might well have been put on in such a pose that the whole symmetry of the original design was spoiled. In those instances in which a head was intended for a vessel being built at a distance from the carver, explicit directions were sent to the master shipwright as to the manner of placing and securing the figure. If the head was sent in several pieces, each joint was distinctly numbered so that the whole could be properly assembled in position.

[31]Wheildon, *Memoirs Solomon Willard.*

[32]Grice Collection; Captain J. D. Henley to Naval Commissioners, August 25, 1828, Navy Department Library.

[33]*Essex Institute Historical Collections,* LXXVIII, 117-157.

[34]Essex Institute, Joseph True Account Book.

[35]*Essex Institute Historical Collections,* LXXVIII, 89.

[36]Clipping at Peabody Museum from an unidentified Salem newspaper.

[37]New York *Directories.*

[38]Putnam, *Salem Vessels and Their Voyages,* II, 58, 130-154; Mss. at Peabody Museum.

[39]Chapelle, *History American Sailing Ships,* figures 30-32; Derby Papers.

[40]Smith, *Revenue Marine,* 6; *Essex Institute Historical Collections,* III, 90; VII, 210; XXXVII, 3.

[41]Hone *Diary,* II, 103.

CHAPTER IV.

[1]Griffiths, *Marine and Naval Architecture,* 392.

[2]Howe and Matthews, *American Clipper Ships,* I, 61.

[3]Ibid., 286.

[4]Ibid., 181.

[5]Ibid., II, 734; Webb's *Plans.*

[6]New York *Herald,* February 9, 1851.

[7]Peabody Museum Collection.

[8]Cutler, *Greyhounds,* 207.

[9]Baltimore *Sun,* 1850-1857. The description of almost every major ship or bark is given in full, sometimes with specifications and details.

[10]*Great Republic,* 6, 22.

[11]Howe and Matthews, *American Clipper Ships,* I, 33, 55, 101, 277.

[12]Ibid., I, 52.

[13]Ibid., I, 214.

[14]Ibid., II, 495.

[15]Ibid., I, 88.

[16]Ibid., II, 569, 663, 718.

[17]Ibid., I, 125; San Francisco Chamber of Commerce; Stevens and Stillman, *Greenman,* 242.

[18]New York City *Directories.*

NOTES AND REFERENCES

19*Great Republic,* 22; Howe and Matthews, *American Clipper Ships,* II, 594, 620; Little, *Rockefeller Folk Art,* 328 picture 329. Some doubt is thrown on the identification of the carving as the work of Gleason by a record that off the River Platte the ship was struck by a pampero which " . . . hove [her] on beam ends; the head was carried away, the bulwarks, galley and round house stove and the cargo shifted". Howe and Matthews, II, 399. It is also to be noted in American Lloyd's *Register of Shipping* that there were two ships of the same name contemporary with McKay's *Minnehaha,* both built in Canada, and a little later an additional two brigs and a schooner. Many of Gleason's bills and letters are in the Fernald & Pettigrew Papers.

20Dow and Robinson, *Sailing Ships of New England,* II, 20; Mason designs, Peabody Museum.

21Clark, *Clipper Ship Era,* 166; MacLean, 8. Mason bills and letters are in the Fernald & Pettigrew Papers.

22Currier, *Ould Newbury,* 414; Belknap, *Arts and Crafts Essex County,* 20; Newburyport *Daily News,* October 20, 1893. A few Wilson bills are in the Hale Papers at Peabody Museum, and a badly decayed figurehead attributed to the Wilson's is owned by the Historical Society of Ould Newbury.

23Newburyport Ship Registers in *Essex Institute Historical Collection,* Vol. LXX et seq.

24Portsmouth, New Hampshire, *Directories;* New England *Directories.*

25Baltimore *Sun,* June 25, 1851; November 27, 1852; October 14, 19, 21, 1853; May 30, 1854; January 12, 1855.

26Fernald & Pettigrew Papers *Samoset.* Cromwell's charge was $100.00 including "Painting & Gilding & Boxing", covering "Bust head Taffrell & Trailboards"; S. M. Dockum also charged:

"For carving one Star	.75
do 15 letters & center piece	3.00
do 2 Cat Head pieces	7.00
do 3 newels	.37
	11.12"

27Ibid., *Empire State.* In 1847 Dodge carved a "Full Figure of Columbus, Trailboards, Chocks & Taffrail $375.00" for the ship *Columbus* for the same builders.

28Ibid., *Western World.* The sketch is not in the papers.

CHAPTER V.

1*Report Commissioner of Navigation,* 1914, Tab. 10.

2Old State House Collection, Boston, Massachusetts; Boston *Directories.*

3Baltimore, Maryland, *Directory,* 1852, advertisement; New York *Directory,* 1868, advertisement.

4*St. Nicholas,* October 1910; De Young Museum Collection.

5Rigg & Bro., 310 Market St., Philadelphia.

6Investigations by C. L. Douglass and Alton Skillin.

7Letters from C. L. Skolfield; New England *Directories.*

8Letters from W. L. Gooding; New England *Directories.*

9*Time,* December 13, 1948.

10Bangor, Maine, *Directories.*

11Letters from Eleanor M. Proctor.

12Thompson, *Captain Nathaniel Lord Thompson,* 94.

13*Antiques,* March, 1935; Letters from M. Victor Safford, M.D.

14Massachusetts Historical Society, Vol. 53; *Oregon Historical Quarterly,* Vol. 24, 132.

[15]Hall, *Report,* 131-136.

[16]San Francisco Maritime Tradesmen, Peabody Museum Mss. Collection.

[17]Letters from Mrs. Grace Lovejoy Faulkner.

[18]Ibid.; Portland, Oregon, *Sunday Telegram,* March 14, 1937.

[19]Buffalo Historical Society *Publications,* Vol. VI, 17 ff; VII, 284 ff.

[20]The Mariners' Museum Collection, OF 63. As examples of the lack of accuracy in the costuming of heads considerable contemporary criticism can be cited. Dr. Bentley on March 22, 1819, mentioned in his *Diary* " . . . . a carved head for the ship *Gouvernour Endicott* [Governor and Lieutenant Governor of Massachusetts from 1641 to 1665] . . . the Costume is that of Gov. Brooks [Governor of Massachusetts from 1816 to 1823] with a modern military dress epaulets & decorations". A Philadelphia newspaper said of Rush "If we were permitted to criticize any part of the work he had brought to such perfection we should mention the feet of his images, which are dressed too much according to modern fashion while the remainder of the clothing is copied from antique statues or taken from fancy. In reality, a Juno, Venus, or Diana in high heel shoes is not in character".

[21]Unidentified newspaper clipping at Peabody Museum.

[22]St. John (N. B.) *Telegram-Journal,* May 1924; *Archives,* New Brunswick Provincial Museum, Scrap Book 36, H. A. Cody, *The Wood Carver of St. John.*

[23]Letters from Holman W. Chaloner to the Author.

[24]The last instructions found on the design of figureheads is in Simpson, *Naval Constructor,* 52. See figure 96.

THE FRIGATE *CONSTITUTION.*

[1]*Laws of the United States in Relation to the Navy . . .,* Washington, 1841, 31-33, "An Act to provide a naval armament".

[2]Humphreys Papers.

[3]Humphreys Letter Book, I; Humphreys letter of February 20, 1795 to Timothy Pickering contained many suggestions which Pickering largely discarded and writing to President Washington, Upham, *Life of Pickering,* 154, made ten suggestions. Of these Washington selected five including *Constitution.*

[4]Humphreys Correspondence. The letter is printed in *Pennsylvania Magazine of History and Biography,* XXXI, 239-40.

[5]Navy Department Mss. Secretary of War to Secretary of Treasury, September 20, 1796.

[6]*Accounts of Expenditures,* 22.

[7]Bentley, *Diary,* II, 224.

[8]Humphreys Letter Book, I, written between May 28 and June 5, 1795 to Secretary of War.

[9]U. S. Naval Academy Museum.

[10]*Antiques,* July 1936, Charles E. Harris, *Figureheads of the Constitution: United States Frigate Constitution,* 11; Hollis, *The Frigate Constitution,* 221.

[11]*Barbary Wars,* V, 17.

[12]Ibid., 57, 58.

[13]Ibid., 81, 93.

[14]Ibid., 51, 94.

[15]Ibid., 51, 81, 82.

[16]Com. John Rodgers Papers, Books of Navy Agent at New York.

[17]Ibid.

[18]This billet was given to the Museum in 1919 by the Eastern Yacht Club. They had received it from Roland C. Nickerson whose father is said to have worked at the

Boston Navy Yard. The billet, full of dry rot was badly repaired with plaster by Russell Treadwell in 1920 and properly restored by an expert wood carver, William A. Robertson, in 1960.

[19]Evans, *Journal,* 36.

[20]Elliott, *Speech,* 20; Citizen, *Biography,* 314.

[21]Citizen, *Biography,* 366.

[22]Ibid., 319.

[23]Ibid., 367.

[24]Citizen, *Biography,* 314 ff; Preble, *Boston Navy Yard,* II, 241-50; the Boston newspapers all give detailed accounts of this phase of the episode.

[25]Citizen, *Biography,* 360.

[26]Navy Department Mss., Ridgley to Navy Commissioners, March 9, 1835.

[27]Ibid., Secretary of Navy to Ridgely, March 13, 1835.

[28]New York *Daily Advertiser,* March 16, 1835. See also *Niles Weekly Register,* March 21, 1835.

[29] Citizen, *Biography,* 360.

[30]Navy Department Mss., Shubrick to Commissioners, January 20, 1842; Commissioners to Shubrick, January 21, 1842.

[31]National Archives, Navy Bureau of Construction and Repair, Repairs of Vessels, I, 84.

[32]Naval Historical Foundation, Snow Collection. Snow to Commandant First Naval District, March 16, 1926; Preble, *Boston Navy Yard,* II, 241 fn.

[33]Snow Collection quoting Dialogue's offer June 23, 1876.

[34]*United States Frigate Constitution,* 11.

[35]The first Jackson figure, Beecher body - Dodge cranium, when removed from the frigate in 1846 was given to the Fowles (Boston *Herald,* July 25, 1920), carvers of the second Jackson figure. It was purchased by Jonathan Bowers (Boston *Herald,* October 21, 1897) and set up in his amusement park at Willowdale, near Lowell, Massachusetts on July 2, 1861. (Clipping from unidentified Lowell newspaper, July 4, 1861). His sons sold it to a New York antique dealer, Max Williams, who in turn sold it at auction in the Anderson Galleries, New York to William B. Leeds, Jr., (*Boston Transcript,* April 21, 1928), who gave it to the Seawanhaka Yacht Club. That organization loaned the figurehead to the Marine Museum of New York where it is today. The whereabouts of the Beecher cranium is not known.

The second Jackson figure has passed through fewer hands. When it was removed from the frigate in 1874 it was set up in the Philadelphia Navy Yard as an ornament. The next year it was transferred to the United States Naval Academy at Annapolis (Preble, *Boston Navy Yard,* II. Preble was commandant at Philadelphia at the time).

Bibliography

BOOKS.

ANONYMOUS.
Laws of the United States in Relation to the Navy . . . Washington, 1841.
U.S. Frigate Constitution. Washington, 1932.
A New Book of Ornaments . . . in . . . Carving . . . Ships. London, 1799.
Catalogue of the . . . Rogers Collection of Ship Models . . . in U. S. Naval Academy. Annapolis, 1954.
Ship Figureheads and Other Wood Carving Art in the Nautical Collection of the State Street Trust Co. Boston, n.d.
Galionsfiguren. Altonaer Museum, 1961.
AUGUIER, PHILIPPE. Pierre Puget, Décorateur et Mariniste. Paris, n.d.
BELKNAP, HENRY W. Artists and Craftsmen of Essex County. Salem, 1927.
BOSTON RECORDS COMMISSION. Reports. Boston, 1876.
CAPE COD ADVANCEMENT PLAN. Ship's Figureheads of Old Cape Cod. Hyannis, 1936.
CAPPON, LESTER J. AND DUFF, STELLA F. Virginia Gazette Index, 1736-80. Williamsburg, 1950.
CHANDLER, CHARLES LYON. Early Shipbuilding in Pennsylvania, 1683-1812. Princeton, 1932.
CHAPELLE, HOWARD IRVING. The Baltimore Clipper. Salem, 1930; The History of American Sailing Ships. New York, 1935.
CHRISTENSEN, ERWIN O. Early American Wood Carving. New York, 1952.
CITIZEN OF NEW YORK. Biographical Notice of Com. Jesse D. Elliott . . . and a History of the Figurehead of the United States Frigate Constitution. Philadelphia, 1835.
CLARK, ARTHUR H. The Clipper Ship Era. New York, 1911.
CLARK, WILLIAM BELL, Lambert Wickes. New Haven, 1932; Gallant John Barry, New York, 1938.
COMMERCE DEPARTMENT. Report of Commissioner of Navigation. Washington, 1914.
CURRIER, JOHN J. Ship-building on the Merrimac. Newburyport, 1877; Ould Newbury. Boston, 1896.
CUTLER, CARL C. Greyhounds of the Sea. New York, 1930.
DOW, GEORGE FRANCIS AND ROBINSON, JOHN. Sailing Ships of New England. Salem, 1922-28.
DUNLAP, WILLIAM. History of Arts of Design in the United States. New York, 1834. (Dover reprint)
ESSEX INSTITUTE. Old Time Ships of Salem. Salem, 1917.
EVANS, AMOS A. Journal Kept on Board the United States Frigate Constitution. n.p., 1928.
FORD, W. C., EDITOR. Journals of Continental Congress. Washington, 1904-39.
GOTTESMAN, RITA SUSSWEIN. The Arts and Crafts in New York, 1726-76, New York, 1938; and Vol. II, 1777-99, 1954.
GRIFFITHS, JOHN W. Marine and Naval Architecture. New York, 1850.

HALL, HENRY. *Report of Ship-Building Industry*. Washington, 1884.

HAZARD, SAMUEL. *Register of Pennsylvania*. Philadelphia, 1826-36.

HOLLIS, IRA, N. *The Frigate Constitution*. Boston, 1931.

HOWE, OCTAVIUS T. AND MATTHEWS, FREDERICK C. *American Clipper Ships*. Salem, 1926-27.

JONES, HENRY M. *Ships of Kingston*. Plymouth, 1926.

KIMBALL, FISKE. *Mr. Samuel McIntire, Carver* . . . Portland, Maine, 1940.

KINGSBURY, SUSAN M. *Records of Virginia Company of London*. Washington, 1906-35.

KITTRIDGE, HENRY C. *Shipmasters of Cape Cod*. Boston, 1935.

KRAFT, HERMAN F. *Catalogue of Historic Objects at the United States Naval Academy*. Annapolis, 1925.

LAUGHTON, L. G. CARR. *Old Ships Figure Heads and Sterns*. London, 1925.

LITTLE, NINA FLETCHER. *Abby Aldrich Rockefeller Folk Art Collection*. Williamsburg, 1957.

McKAY, RICHARD C. *Some Famous Sailing Ships and Their Builder Donald McKay*. New York, 1928.

McLEAN, DUNCAN. *Clipper Ships and Packets 1851-1853*. Washington, 1952.

MARVIN, WINTHROP L. *American Merchant Marine, 1620-1902*. New York, 1902.

MATTHEWS, FREDERICK C. *American Merchant Ships, 1850-1900*. Salem, 1930-31.

MARCEAU, HENRI. *Works of William Rush*. Philadelphia, 1937.

Maryland Archives. Baltimore, 1882-

MASON, GEORGE C. *Reminiscences of Newport*. Newport, 1884.

NAVY DEPARTMENT. Bureau of Navigation. *Bulletin No. 134. Tecumseh Number*. Washington, 1930; *Quasi-War Between the United States and France*. Washington, 1935-37; *Barbary Wars* . . . . Washington, 1939-45.

NESSER, ROBERT WILDEN. *The Despatches of Molyneux Shuldham*, Naval History Society, New York, 1913.

PAINE, RALPH D. *Ships and Sailors of Old Salem*. New York, 1919.

PAXON, HENRY D. *Figure Head of Chief Tammany*. Doylestown, 1921.

Pennsylvania Archives. Harrisburg, 1852-.

PERLEY, SIDNEY. *History of Salem*. Salem, 1924.

PINCKNEY, PAULINE A. *American Figureheads and Their Carvers*. New York, 1940.

PORTER, EDWARD G. *Rambles in Old Boston*. Boston, 1887.

PRIME, ALFRED COXE. *Arts and Crafts in Philadelphia, Maryland, and South Carolina*. Walpole Society, 1929.

RICKETSON, DANIEL, *History of New Bedford*. New Bedford, 1858.

ROBINSON, JOHN. *Catalog of Marine Room Peabody Museum*, Salem, 1921.

"A SAILOR". *The Great Republic*. Boston, 1853.

SCHARF, J. THOMAS AND WESTCOTT, THOMPSON. *History of Philadelphia*, Philadelphia, 1884.

SEVERANCE, FRANK. *Historic Figureheads*. Buffalo Historical Society, Buffalo, 1921.

SHEWAN, ANDREW. *The Great Days of Sail*. Boston, 1927.

SIMPSON, GEORGE. *The Naval Constructor*. New York, 1919.

SMITH, CAPTAIN H. D. *Early History of the United States Revenue Marine*. Washington, 1932.

SOLEY, JAMES RUSSELL. *Historical Sketch of the United States Naval Academy*. Washington, 1876,

BIBLIOGRAPHY

SPRAGUE, FRANCES W. *Barnstable and Yarmouth Sea Captains and Ship Owners.* Privately Printed, 1913.

STEVENS, THOMAS A. AND STILLMAN, DR. CHARLES K. *George Greenman & Company, Shipbuilders.* Mystic, 1938.

Suffolk Deeds. Boston, 1880.

SUTHERLAND, WILLIAM. *The Ship-builder's Assistant.* London, 1711.

SWAN, OLIVER G. *Deep Water Days.* Philadelphia, 1929.

THOMPSON, MARGARET J. *Captain Nathaniel Lord Thompson.* Boston, 1937.

TUCKERMAN, BAYARD. *Diary of Philip Hone.* New York, 1889.

UPHAM, C. W. *Life of Timothy Pickering.* Boston, n.d.

WALLACE, FREDERICK WILLIAM. *Wooden Ships and Iron Men.* London, 1924.

WATSON, JOHN F. *Annals of Philadelphia.* Philadelphia, 1868.

WEBB, WILLIAM H. *Plans of Wooden Vessels.* New York, n.d.

WHEILDON, WILLIAM W. *Memoir of Solomon Willard.* Boston, 1865.

DIRECTORIES.

Baltimore.

Bangor.

Boston.

Charleston, South Carolina.

New England.

New York.

Philadelphia.

Portsmouth, New Hampshire.

Salem.

San Francisco.

MAGAZINES.

(Only the more important articles are specifically noted.)

American Architect.

December 1929.

American Neptune.

I, 82. Walter Muir Whitehill; "A Figurehead of Talma".

III, 35. Alexander Crosby Brown; "Paddle Box Decorations of American Sound Steamboats".

VII, 255. Eugene S. Ferguson; "The Figurehead of the United States Frigate Constellation".

IX, 72. Charles H. P. Copeland; "A Figurehead of Talma".

Antiques.

January 1932. Fiske Kimball; "Estimate of McIntire."

December 1931. Mabel M. Swan; "Revised Estimate of McIntire".

March 1935. Mabel M. Swan; "Artisan Leaders of 1788".

March 1935. M. Victor Safford; "John Haley Bellamy".

July 1936, Charles E. Harris; "Figureheads of the Constitution".

June 1938. Leroy L. Thwing; "Four Carving Skillins".

Arts and Decorations.

September 1932. Edith S. Watson; "Figureheads from Old Ships Rest in Modern Gardens".

Century, The

August 1916. Victoria Hayward; "Figureheads of the Old Square Riggers".

Cosmopolitan, The
April 1893. Robert G. Denig; "Historic Figure Heads".
Craftsman, The
Volume V.
Daughters of the American Revolution.
October 1927. Jenny Girton Walker; "The Ship Figurehead in American History".
Essex Institute Historical Collections. Salem, 1859-
Home Journal, The
August 1899. Theodore Waters; "The First American Sculptor".
Illustrated America.
January 1917. W. C. van Antwerp; "Figureheads of Famous Old Men of War".
International Studio.
September 1922. "Garden of Figureheads".
September 1929. "Nadleman Ship Figureheads".
Leslie's.
December 17, 1859.
Literary Digest.
May 19, 1917. "Reviving the Figurehead".
Motor Boating.
October 1928.
Museum, The, Newark, New Jersey.
Volume 2 and 3. 1928-1932. "Curious History of the Jackson Figure Head".
New England Historical Genealogical Register.
Volume XXII, 393.
Outlook.
January 27, 1915. David H. Wasson; "The Silent Pilots".
Pennsylvania Magazine of History and Biography.
Volume XXXI, 239. "William Rush to Joshua Humphreys".
Popular Mechanics.
May 1932.
Putnam's Historical Magazine.
December 1893. D. Turner; "The Frigate Constitution and its Figure Heads".
Rudder, The
December 1919. Robert G. Skerrett; "Time Honored Practice of Ornamenting Ships".
Sea Breezes.
July 1932.
Seamens Church Institute of New York.
Various short articles.
Scientific American.
August 7, 1909. "The Figurehead and its Story".
Saint Nicholas.
October 1910. Day Allen Willey; "Old Figureheads".
Travel.
July 1935. Ethel Romig Fuller; "Guardians of the Windjammers".
United States Naval Institute.
May-June 1914. Charles F. Preston; "Tamanend vs. Tecumseh".
November 1927. Constance Lathop; "A Vanishing Naval Tradition".
November 1927. Secretary's Notes.

BIBLIOGRAPHY

Vogue.
> December 1932.

Yachting.
> January 1917. Victoria Hayward; "Figureheads and Stern Work on Ships".

MANUSCRIPTS.

ESSEX INSTITUTE.
> Custom House Papers.
> Derby Papers.
> McIntire Papers.
> True Account Book.
> Ward Papers.

HISTORICAL SOCIETY OF PENNSYLVANIA.
> Joseph Carson Receipt Books.
> Connarroe Collection.
> William Davidson Diary.
> Levi Hollingsworth Papers.
> Joshua Humphreys Papers.
> James Logan Papers.
> John Norris Papers.
> John Reynall Papers.
> Com. John Rodgers Papers.
> William Rush Bills.
> Wharton-Storey Papers.
> Charles Wharton Papers.

MASSACHUSETTS HISTORICAL SOCIETY.
> Caleb Davis Papers.
> Wolcott Papers.

NATIONAL ARCHIVES.
> Bureau of Construction and Repair Files and Plans of Ships.

NAVAL HISTORICAL FOUNDATION.
> Admiral Elliott Snow Collection.

NAVY DEPARTMENT.
> Subject File.
> Area File.
> G. H. Preble Ms., *History of Boston Navy Yard.*

PEABODY MUSEUM.
> Carleton Norwood Papers.
> Carver's File.
> Custom House Papers.
> Fernald & Pettigrew Papers.
> Josiah Fox Papers.
> Hale Papers.
> Benjamin Shreve Papers.
> Joseph Waters Papers.

MISCELLANEOUS.
> Admirals Despatches, Public Records Office, London.
> Deering Mss., Ould Newbury Historical Society.
> Hudson Papers, New York Public Library.

Massachusetts State Archives, Boston.
Official Correspondence, Navy Department Library.
Provincial Papers, Pennsylvania State Library.
Records, Philadelphia Custom House.
Nathaniel Shaw Papers, Yale University Library.
Stephen Girard Papers, Girard College.

COLLECTIONS OF FIGUREHEADS.

Buffalo Historical Society, Buffalo.
Bourne Museum, New Bedford.
India House, New York.
India Wharf Rats Club, Boston.
Kendall Whaling Museum, Sharon.
"Long John Silver", Gravesend, England.
Mariners' Museum, Newport News.
Masonic Temple, Philadelphia.
Museum of the City of New York.
Museum of Fine Arts, Boston.
Mystic Seaport, Mystic.
Naval Academy, Annapolis.
Old State House, Boston.
Peabody Museum, Salem.
Penobscot Marine Museum, Searsport.
Seamen's Church Institute, New York.
State Street Bank and Trust Company, Boston.
de Young Museum, San Francisco.

NEWSPAPERS.

Maryland Gazette, Annapolis and Baltimore.
Federal Gazette, Baltimore.
Niles Weekly Register, Baltimore.
Boston Gazette.
Evening Post, Boston.
South Carolina Gazette, Charleston.
Newburyport Daily News.
New York Daily Advertiser.
New York Herald.
New York Mercury.
American Daily Advertiser, Philadelphia.
Philadelphia Daily Advertiser.
Evening Bulletin, Philadelphia.
Sunday Telegram, Portland, Maine.

PHOTOGRAPH AND SCRAP BOOK COLLECTIONS.

C. L. Douglass, Esqr., Bath, Maine.
Myers Collection, New York Public Library.
Staff Collection, Room 121, New York Public Library.
Peabody Museum, Salem.

BIBLIOGRAPHY

PLANS OF VESSELS AND MODELS.

Admiralty Collection, National Maritime Museum, London.
R. C. Anderson, Esqr., Greenwich, England.
Atheneum, Portsmouth, New Hampshire.
Independence Hall, Philadelphia.
Navy Department, Washington.
Peabody Museum, Salem.
de Young Museum, San Francisco.

List of American Shipcarvers

THIS LIST includes the names of only those carvers who definitely did work for vessels as a major part of their business. Other carvers, men who did such pieces as cabinet work, picture frames, coach and chair work, or architectural carvings are not listed, even though they may have occasionally done some piece of shipcarving.

California.

    San Francisco.

Edward Lovejoy	1857 b - 1917 d
William Gereau	1858 w - 1875 d
Louis A. Haehnlen	1859 w
Thomas Carroll	1860 w
Tarleton B. Earl	1860 w - 1870 w
Mon Hon	1861 w
John Farrell	1868 w - 1870 w
James W. Telfer	1870 w
F. L. Weaver	1875 w
Paul Hubbard	1876 w - 1877 w
Benjamin Luce	1876 w - 1877 w

Connecticut.

    Darien.

Dexter K. Cole	1833 w

    Mystic.

        John Colby

        James Campbell

    New London.

Joseph B. Neal	1854 w

District of Columbia.

Edward Gottier	1806 w
. . . . . Concklin	1809 w

Louisiana.
    New Orleans
        J. Gastal   1866 w

Maine.
    Bangor.
        W. L. Seavey   1834 b - 1912 d
        Thomas Seavey   1843 w - 1886 d
    Bath.
        Nathaniel Winsor   1820 w
        Samuel D. Wyman   1828 b
        C. A. L. Sampson   1848 w - 1881 d
        Cyrus Ingalls   1856 w
        G. B. McLain & Co.   1856 w
        Wm. Southworth   1880 w - 1909 d
        . . . . . Newcomb   1880 ca.
        Woodbury Potter   1880 ca. - 1893 w
    Belfast.
        F. W. Gilbert   1853 w
        Gilbert & Worcester   1853 w - 1889 w
        D. R. Procter   1856 w
        J. C. Abbott   1856 w
    Blue Hill.
        T. M. Lord   1856 w
    Bucksport.
        Colby, Emery & Co.   1868 w
        Leon B. Pratt   1878 w
    Camden.
        Jeremiah C. Cushing   1859 w
        Henry M. Prince   1885 w
    Damariscotta.
        Emery Jones
        Edbury Hatch   1849 b - 1935 d
    Freeport.
        Emery Jones   1827 b - 1908 d
    Hallowell.
        Alexander Currier
        Alvin Drew   1856 w

Kittery.

T. W. Coutis	1722 w	
Thomas More	1720 w	
George Naber	1722 w	
James Titcomb	1722 w	

Machias.

H. W. Chaloner	1851 b	
James Todd	1860 w	

Millbridge.

S. L. Treat	1868 w	

Newcastle.

William Southworth	1856 w - 1881 w	
Southworth & Jones	1856 w	

Portland.

Nathan Chapman	1834 w	
Edward S. Griffin	1834 b - 1928 d	
A. Chapman	1849 w	
Nahorn Littlefield	1856 w - 1878 w	
Charles H. Littlefield	1858 w	
Francis A. Littlefield	1858 w	
Nathan Littlefield	1863 w	
Theodore Johnson	1868 w - 1878 w	
J. P. Merrill	1878 w	
W. A. Simmons	1878 w	

Richmond.

Richard Mace	1856 w	
Stoddard & McLaughlin	1856 w	

Rockland.

James Todd		
J. E. Verrill	1839 w - 1878 w	
S. L. Treat	1860 w	

Thomaston.

Harvey Counce	1821 w	
R. H. Counce & Co.	1856 w - 1878 w	

Waldoboro.

Samuel D. Wyman	1828 b	

Maryland.

Annapolis.

Henry Crouch	1760 w			

Baltimore.

John Brown	1789 w	-	1804	w
Joseph Bias	1796 w			
Joseph Brieschaft	1804 w			
Thomas Appleton	1824 w			
Reuben Macy	1831 w	-	1838	d
Robert B. Macy	1831 w			
Harold & Randolph	1835 w			
Samuel Hubbart	1840 w	-	1852	w
James Campbell	1851 w			
James Mullen	1852 w	-	1858	w
James Mullen of O	1854 w	-	1858	w
James T. Randolph	1850 w	-	1857	w
William Seward	1858 w			
Bernard Van Wynen	1853 w	-	1858	w
Richard Callahan	1868 w	-	1875	w

Solomon's.

. . . . . Olson	1880 w			

Woolford.

W. Hammond Skinner	1860 w	-	1900	w
Edward Skinner	1890 w			
John Skinner	1890 w			

Massachusetts.

Boston.

Richard Knight	1623 b	-	1689	w
Edward Budd	1668 w	-	1689	w
George Robinson	1681 w	-	1737	d
John Welch	1711 b	-	1789	d
Simeon Skillin	1716 b	-	1778	d
Joshua Bowles	1720 b	-	1794	d
Samuel More	1736 w			
Samuel Skillin	1742 b	-	1816	d
John Skillin	1746 b	-	1800	d

Simeon Skillin	1757 b	- 1806 d
Isaac Du Pee	1758 w	
Thomas Lucus	1760 w	
Thomas Richardson (Head Builder)	1781 w	- 1796 w
Solomon Willard	1783 b	- 1861 d
Joseph Robertson (Head Builder)	1791 w	- 1796 w
Richardson & Swift (Head Builder)	1796 w	
Samuel Skillin	1796 w	
Thomas Dilloway	1799 w	
John Richardson (Head Builder)	1800 w	
Edmund Raymond	1805 w	- 1806 w
Laban S. Beecher	1805 b	- 1876 d
Raymond & Fowle	1807 w	- 1813 w
Isaac Fowle	1813 w	- 1832 w
John W. Mason	1814 b	- 1866 d
Isaac Fowle & Co.	1832 w	- 1853 w
Samuel L. Winsor	1832 w	- 1848 w
Levi L. Cushing	1836 w	
C. A. L. Sampson	1847 w	
S. W. Gleason & Sons	1847 w	
William H. Brown	1847 w	
Stoddard & McLaughlin	1852 w	- 1863 w
Chapman & Hastings	1854 w	
W. G. Gleason	1854 w	
J. D. & W. H. Fowle	1854 w	- 1862 w
N. Stoddard	1859 w	
William Lindsay	1859 w	
T. J. White & Co.	1859 w	- 1868 w
J. D. & J. H. Fowle	1863 w	- 1864 w
McIntyre & Gleason	1863 w	- 1871 w
John D. Fowle	1865 w	- 1869 w
E. W. Hastings	1865 w	- 1878 w
Joseph J. Doherty	1872 w	- 1908 w
W. H. Rumney	1873 w	
Herbert Gleason	1871 w	- 1878 w
Hastings & Gleason	1878 w	- 1896 w

Charlestown.
    Oliver Holden
    Thomas Lucas   1789 w
    Woodbury Gerrish   1853 w
    J. W. & A. Lees   1868 w
Duxbury.
    Nathaniel Winsor   1820 w
East Boston.
    D. W. Lewis Hunt   1845 w
Gloucester.
    D. R. Proctor   1856 w
    S. Merchant & Co.   1868 w
    Samuel Elwell   1869 w
Haverhill.
    G. B. McClain & Co.   1842 w - 1847 w
Ipswich.
    William A. Robertson   1935 w - 1940 w
Mattapoisett.
    Henry J. Purrington   1868 w
Meridan.
    W. H. Brown   1842 w
New Bedford.
    Alvin Coleman   1836 w
    Hezekiah Coleman   1836 w
Newburyport.
    William Davenport   1738 b - 1762 w
    Joseph Wilson   1798 w
    James W. Wilson   1825 b - 1893 d
    Albert H. Wilson   1828 b
Salem.
    Leaman Beadle   1680 b - 1717 d
    Joseph McIntire   1747 b - 1825 d
    Samuel McIntire   1757 b - 1811 d
    Samuel Field McIntire   1780 b - 1819 d
    Joseph McIntire Jr.   - 1852 d
    Edward Dorr (Head Builder) 1812 w
    Joseph True   1816 b - 1866 d

Michigan.
    Detroit.
        J. T. Melchers

New Hampshire.
    Portsmouth.

William Deering	1706 b	
William Deering	1741 b -	1799 w
John Bellamy	1836 b -	1914 d
Woodbury Gerrish	-	1868 d
Joseph Henderson	1860 w	
S. M. Dockum	1868 w	
Ivah W. Spinney		

New York.
    Brooklyn.

Van Wynen & Brother	1871 w	

    Buffalo.

Alexander Lowery	1844 w	
Alexander Ames	1847 w	

    New York City.

George Warburton	1729 w	
Henry Hardcastle	1759 w	
Stephen Dwight	1755 w -	1763 w
Samuel Skillin	1785 w -	1818 d
John Skillin	1793 w	
Simeon Skillin	1792 w -	1821 w
Daniel N. Train	1799 w -	1812 w
John Taylor	1803 w -	1815 w
William Cook	1804 w -	1815 w
Skillin & Dodge	1804 w -	1810 w
Jeremiah Dodge	1804 w	
Train & Collins	1806 w	
Sharpe & Ellis	1810 w	
C. N. Sharpe	1817 w	
Dodge & Sharpe	1820 w -	1821 w
Heron & Weeden	1825 w	
Wm. S. Drawbridge	1830 w	

James Heron	1830 w		
Heron & Macy	1830 w		
Reuben Macy	1830 w		
Robert H. Macy	1830 w		
Thomas Milliard Jr.	1830 w		
Jacob Anderson & Co.	1830 w	-	1836 w
John L. Cromwell	1831 w	-	1859 w
Jeremiah Dodge & Son	1833 w	-	1835 w
Morrell & Morriss	1834 w		
Charles J. Dodge	1835 w	-	1859 w
John Weedon	1836 w		
Dodge & Anderson	1836 w	-	1847 w
Cromwell & Harold	1841 w	-	1852 w
George H. Buck	1845 w		
Jacob S. Anderson	1847 w	-	1857 w
Stratton & Morrell	1845 w		
Willett H. Morrell	1845 w		
T. V. Brooks	1852 w	-	1857 w
John Fraser	1852 w		
Joseph Stratton	1852 w		
John Weedon	1852 w	-	1857 w
Hoffman & Maurer	1853 w		
Wilson & Schaettler	1853 w	-	1854 w
Kessel & Hartung	1857 w		
Winter Lundmark	1857 w		
J. S. Anderson & Son	1857 w	-	1858 w
John W. Anderson	1858 w		
A. N. Wooster	1860 w		
Joseph Bowers	1860 w		
Charles McColley	1868 w		
Kurtz & Co.	1873 w		
Samuel A. Robb	1880 w		
Gustave Guiterman			

Pennsylvania.
  Philadelphia.

Robert Mullard	1709 w	-	1722 w
Anthony Wilkinson	1729 w	-	1765 d

William Hunt	1734 w - 1737 w
Henry Wells	1746 w - 1748 w
Bryant Wilkinson	1749 w
Samuel Harding	1754 w - 1758 w
Samuel Skillin	1765 w - 1784 w
Edward Cutbush	1770 w - 1790 w
Samuel Cutbush	1785 w
William Lake	1785 w
William Rush	1756 b - 1833 d
John Merriam	1791 w
Benjamin Rush	1793 w
David Cather	1793 w
William Griffith	1793 w
Thomas Milliard	1795 w
Richard Watson	1798 w
John Brown	1798 w
Abraham Collins	1810 w
James Leconey	1813 w
John Rush	1814 w
..... Bids	1819 w
Charles Milliard	1833 w
James Milliard	1833 w - 1856 w
William Lingard	1856 w
Samuel Sailor	1858 w - 1875 w

Rhode Island.

William Allin	1757 w

South Carolina.

Charleston.

Henry Burnett	1750 w
George Harris	1766 w
Phillip Witherstone	1773 w
Henry Hainsdorf	1776 w
John Parkinson	1777 w
Cotten & Statler	1796 w
William Gardner	1799 w

Virginia.
    Norfolk.
        William Luke   1800 w
        Henry Wells   1800 w
        Frank Benson   1801 w

Wisconsin.
        Laban S. Beecher   1805 b - 1876 d

New Brunswick.
    Saint John.
        Edward Charters   1849 w
        John Rogerson   1837 b - 1925 d

Quebec.
    Ste. Anne de Beaupre
        Louis Jobin   1925 w
    St. Roche
        Jean-Baptiste Côté   1865 w - 1880 w

Index

INDEX

INDEX